D1567986

the breast cancer cookbook

the breast cancer cookbook

Over 100 easy recipes to nourish and boost health during and after treatment

Mohammed Keshtgar
Consultant Breast Cancer Specialist, The Royal Free Hospital London

with Dr. Claire Robertson
and Dr. Miriam Dwek

FOREWORD BY
Alastair M. Thompson
BSc(Hons), MB ChB, MD, FRCSEd of The University of Texas MD
Anderson Cancer Center, Houston

Recipes by Emily Jonzen
Photography by Jan Baldwin

quadrille

Recipe notes

All recipes have been analyzed for their calorie, total fat, saturated fat, sugar, and salt contents per 100 g and per portion to ensure they are appropriate for inclusion in a healthy balanced diet.

All spoon measures are level unless otherwise stated:
1 tsp = ⅙ fl oz spoon;
1 Tbsp = ½ fl oz spoon.

Please use fresh herbs and freshly ground pepper unless otherwise suggested.

Use medium eggs unless otherwise suggested. Anyone who is pregnant or in a vulnerable health group should avoid recipes that use raw egg whites or lightly cooked eggs.

If using the zest of citrus fruit, buy unwaxed fruit.

Timings are guidelines for fan-assisted ovens. If you are using a conventional oven, set your oven temperature approximately 59°F (15°C, 1 Gas mark) higher. Use an oven thermometer to check the temperature.

Contents

Foreword

We are what we eat. At a time when breast cancer affects one in eight women in the United States and so looms large on our individual and communal horizon, turning to reconsider the modern lifestyle, especially how we prepare, eat and enjoy food is a great idea.

Some one in four breast cancers may develop influenced by the food we eat, drinking alcohol and, after the menopause, weight gain. Most of us do not have the high calorie needs of athletes and so we need to balance our intake with the amount of exercise we manage to do. Thus, the balance between the quality and quantity of food and drink we enjoy versus energy expenditure can affect the development of breast cancer, health during treatment for the disease and long-term survivorship. Some treatments reduce our ability to taste food normally, make the mouth sensitive or swallowing uncomfortable. Others upset the normal workings of our insides, resulting in diarrhea or constipation—either of which can disrupt normal life. And yet, weight gain as a consequence of some of the medicines offered, lack of exercise due to fatigue and, for some, comfort eating can bring added complexity.

What can we as individuals, friends and families do to counter these influences on developing cancer and the consequences of treatments? Finding good, nutritious food and presenting that food in a tasty and attractive way has the potential to reduce the chance of breast cancer and for those who have been afflicted, improve the quality of life and maybe, just maybe, tip things in our favor long term.

So, browse this book. Go on, choose a recipe and try it out! You will find the combination of ingredients are simple to put together, take little time or effort to combine or cook and make a balanced and nutritious dish. Above all, they also taste great and support you on the road towards a healthier, happier lifestyle in the future. Enjoy!

Alastair M. Thompson BSc(Hons), MB ChB, MD, FRCSEd
Professor of Surgery and Breast Cancer Specialist, University of Texas MD Anderson Cancer Center, Houston Texas

Introduction

"I have found that as soon as a patient is informed of a breast cancer diagnosis, the majority like to take an active role in their treatment. Diet and lifestyle are two aspects they can modify immediately and with relative ease."

You may be reading this book because you have been diagnosed with breast cancer, either recently or a while ago, or you may feel that you have a higher risk of developing it, perhaps because you have one or more relatives with breast cancer. Or you may be fit and well and simply are concerned about your health in some way. I was motivated to write this book in collaboration with my colleagues as I have become increasingly convinced that diet and lifestyle are contributing factors to the development of cancer.

Over the years, I have met and treated countless women, and some men, with breast cancer. In my experience, when a patient is informed of their breast cancer diagnosis, after a short period of getting over the shock of the news, the majority would like to take an active role in their treatment. They find loss of control difficult to bear and they would like to regain that control. I am asked to advise them on what they can do to help them fight the disease. Diet and lifestyle are two aspects that they can modify immediately, and with relative ease.

Many feel empowered to take responsibility for themselves. This also helps them to go into fight mode and psychologically feel better about themselves and their treatment. This experience is coupled with the fact that there have been major advances in the effective treatment of breast cancer. Being diagnosed with the disease is not all doom and gloom and the majority of our patients make a full recovery after treatment.

Approximately 30% of cancers and their sequelae are influenced by five behavioral risk factors: dietary intake, high body mass index, low fruit and vegetable intake, lack of physical activity, tobacco, and alcohol use. No single factor is causal or protective, and many factors interplay in some way.

Eating and drinking are an integral part of our lives. We are what we eat and our lifestyle can contribute to our general wellbeing and also to the development of cancer. We are also able to modify our diet and therefore alter the risk of developing cancer, including breast cancer. Changes in dietary patterns are not only related to a reduction in the risk of developing breast cancer, there is also evidence that breast cancer recurrence rates are reduced and survival is improved when patients diagnosed and treated for breast cancer adopt a healthy lifestyle.

It is estimated that as many as 9% of cancer cases may be prevented by individuals changing their diet. Research also suggests that about 5% could be avoided by maintaining a healthy body weight. Of course, it takes time to change your diet, certainly for you to be content with that change, and for it to become lasting. If, for example, your diet has been low in fruit and vegetables, yet high in sugary foods such as cakes and cookies, and you are looking to reverse that balance, it will take time for your appetite to adapt … but adapt it will, if you are motivated and persistent. It follows that the consequent improvement to your health and wellbeing will also take time.

What is breast cancer?

Normal tissues are made up of cells of different types that are arranged to form an organ, such as a breast. It is the DNA that controls what happens in the cell. When the DNA changes (a process called mutation), it leads to cells starting to grow out of control and ultimately results in cancer.

Breast cancer is by far the commonest cancer in women. Worldwide, more than 1.5 million women are diagnosed with breast cancer every year. The majority of women develop breast cancer after their menopause, but about two out of every ten patients are under 50 years of age. The risk of developing breast cancer for a woman who lives to 85 years of age in the UK is currently 1 in 8. Thanks to significant developments in medicine and the biomedical sciences, more than 85% of the women diagnosed with breast cancer remain alive and well 5 years after their diagnosis.

Breast cancer risk factors

Breast cancer is a multifactorial disease and although its causes and natural history remain unclear, epidemiological research indicates that genetic, biological, environmental, dietary, and lifestyle aspects are among the risk factors for the disease.

Key risk factors include the individual's reproductive history. For example, exposure to a greater number of menstrual cycles, that is to say early-age onset of menstruation and late-age onset of menopause, as well as having fewer children, are risk factors. Being overweight and consumption of alcohol are also among the risk factors. The underlying reason for this increased risk is the exposure to the female sex hormone estrogen; this hormone is known to bind to a receptor molecule in breast cells and drive cell division.

Increased cell division increases the chance of an individual developing breast cancer. Preventing long-term exposure to estrogen reduces the risk of breast cancer.

HRT (hormone replacement therapy) involves taking female sex hormones to replace hormones that your ovaries no longer produce after menopause. It is mainly taken in order to reduce the symptoms of menopause like hot flashes and lack of energy. Taking HRT increases the risk of developing breast and ovarian cancer. The longer you take HRT, the more your breast cancer risk increases. The good news is that if you are already taking HRT and have decided to stop, your risk of cancer development will revert back to normal within 5 years of stopping it.

Aside from reproductive history, inheriting a faulty (mutated) gene is responsible for approximately 5 to 10% of all breast cancers. The most common of these are the BRCA1 and BRCA2 genes. If you have a faulty gene, it doesn't mean you'll definitely develop breast cancer, but you are at a higher risk. Out of every 100 women with a faulty gene, between 50 and 85 of them will develop breast cancer in their lifetime.

Gene testing, which is done by a blood test, can be offered to you, if you have a high-risk family history of breast or ovarian cancer. This can include close relatives of women with a faulty gene, and women with a strong family history of breast cancer. It is preferable that a living family member with breast or ovarian cancer is available for gene testing, however it is possible to do the test if this is not the case.

If you are found to have a faulty gene, the options include undergoing preventative mastectomy, as was the case with Angelina Jolie, which significantly raised the public awareness about gene testing. The other options include prevention by the use of antihormone drugs such as Tamoxifen. Alternatively, you may choose to opt for regular yearly checkups and undergo active surveillance.

Treatment for breast cancer

If you have been diagnosed with breast cancer, various treatments may be offered to you, depending on the features related to you and your cancer. These treatment options include surgery, which may involve removing the lump (lumpectomy) or the whole breast (mastectomy).

Radiotherapy involves using high energy x-rays to kill cancer cells, and some patients may receive this treatment after breast

> "Breast cancer risk factors include exposure to a greater number of menstrual cycles, taking HRT, having fewer children, lack of breast feeding, being overweight, consumption of alcohol, and inheriting a faulty gene."

"Over the years, there have been significant advances in the diagnosis and treatment of breast cancer. These include advances in surgery, radiotherapy, anti-hormone medications, and chemotherapy."

surgery. It involves coming to hospital on a daily basis for up to 4 to 5 weeks and receiving the treatment by lying under the x-ray delivery machine for a few minutes per treatment.

Hormonal treatment works by giving a drug that prevents the female sex hormone estrogen from stimulating cancer cells. This treatment is recommended if the cancer is hormone responsive, which can be checked under the microscope after surgery.

Chemotherapy is the use of drugs to kill cancer cells and there are a number of chemotherapy drugs that can be used alone or in combination for the treatment of breast cancer.

This treatment is usually delivered intravenously at three-weekly intervals (cycles) and is extremely effective. Many individuals tolerate the treatment well and are able to eat normally during chemotherapy, however a small minority may suffer one or more side effects that can impact on their eating. So let's explore this in more detail.

Chemotherapy can affect the appetite. This may happen soon after the delivery of the drugs and may be associated with feeling sick (nausea) and vomiting, which can be controlled by anti-sickness medication. These symptoms usually improve within a few days of each treatment. It is important to eat regularly (albeit small portions) and keep well hydrated by drinking plenty of water.

The other possible side effect of chemotherapy is soreness of the mouth, which can lead to discomfort during eating. It may be helpful to avoid consuming spicy, acidic, and very hot foods until the underlying problem is settled. Some patients have reported discomfort whilst swallowing owing to this problem and the use of soups and semisolid foods would be helpful in this situation.

"Chemotherapy is the use of drugs to kill cancer cells. Many individuals tolerate the treatment well and are able to eat normally, however a minority suffer a few side effects that can impact on their eating. There are effective ways to overcome these side effects."

Some patients who receive chemotherapy may experience a change in their taste sensation, finding that most of their usual foods taste somewhat bland. This is due to the effect of chemotherapy on tastebuds. The inclusion of strongly flavored foods during this period may help to overcome the problem.

Chemotherapy can also affect bowel habits, resulting in either diarrhea or constipation. Loose motions may occur due to the effect of the chemotherapy drugs on the lining of the gut, and it is imperative that you drink plenty of fluid to avoid dehydration during this period.

On the other hand, constipation can happen due to the lack of physical activity and also as a side effect of some of the supportive drugs, like painkillers and anti-sickness medication. Drinking plenty of fluid and eating high-fiber foods such as fruit and vegetables should help to alleviate this problem.

Finally, you may be surprised to know that most patients are inclined to put on, rather than lose, a bit of weight during chemotherapy. This is due to a combination of factors, including reduced mobility and exercise, comfort eating, and as a side effect to the family of drugs called steroids, which lead to fluid retention in the body and increase the appetite. It is important to stick to a well-balanced diet, as described in this book, during this period. Most patients are able to shed the excess weight easily after completion of their chemotherapy, by increasing their daily physical activity and continuing to eat a healthy diet.

Diet and lifestyle influences

Global studies exploring geographical differences in breast cancer incidence have taught us a lot about diet and lifestyle influences. For example, in Northern Europe the percentage of breast cancer cases is about three times higher than in Eastern Asia. Studies of populations that migrate from areas with low breast cancer risk (such as Japan) to areas of high breast cancer risk (the US, for instance) have shown that the risk of developing the disease increases to approximately that of the host nation within a few generations. Clearly, this suggests that dietary, lifestyle, and environmental factors are contributing factors to the risk of developing breast cancer.

Moreover, epidemiological evidence suggests that the Mediterranean diet could reduce the risk of breast cancer. A comprehensive study of approximately 330,000 women in 10 European countries over an 11-year period ending in the year 2000 showed that adherence to a Mediterranean diet excluding alcohol was related to a modest risk reduction of breast cancer in postmenopausal women.

Our own research is focusing on the effects of diet and lifestyle on the recurrence of breast cancer. We are coordinating the largest dietary study to date of breast cancer patients within the UK. The study is called DietCompLyf and includes over 3,000 patients from 56 National Health Service hospitals. We expect that the study will start to yield results in the very near future.

Body weight
There is a definite link between body mass index (BMI) and breast cancer. Being overweight and having excess weight around the stomach (central adiposity) is linked to the incidence of postmenopausal breast cancer. Weight gain after the age of 20 and high weight gain during mid adulthood also increase the risk of breast cancer. The association seems to be more pronounced for breast cancer diagnosed before or at the age of 50, so it is important to keep fit and avoid weight gain during this period.

Without doubt, eating a balanced diet and keeping active will help to maintain a healthy weight and reduce the risk of breast cancer.

Physical activity
Regular physical activity can improve health by helping to control weight, reducing the risk of heart disease, and keeping the blood pressure steady. It also promotes psychological wellbeing by increasing the levels of endorphins (the "happy hormones") in the body.

Physical activity also helps to keep bones strong and healthy. This holds true particularly with weight-bearing exercises like walking and light jogging. This type of activity is particularly useful for breast cancer patients who are on the specialized antihormone medications known as aromatase inhibitors, the long-term use of which can predispose to osteoporosis.

Although this is a difficult area to investigate, several studies have confirmed the link between physical activity and reduced risk of cancer, in particular breast and bowel cancer. The indication that a high level of physical activity reduces the risk of postmenopausal breast cancer is particularly notable.

The Surgeon General recommends moderate-intensity physical activity for at least 30 minutes, on all or more days a week, or at least 20 minutes of high-intensity exercise for three or more days a week.

Alcohol consumption

Alcohol consumption has been linked to an increase in both the risk of developing breast cancer and the likelihood of breast cancer recurrence. This is independent of the type of alcoholic drink consumed and menopausal status. Since the early 1980s, numerous studies have examined this link.

Even for light drinkers, there appears to be a moderate increased risk. That risk increases with the volume of alcohol consumed. For women who have three or more alcoholic drinks per day there is a 40 to 50% elevated risk of breast cancer.

The exact mechanism by which alcohol raises breast cancer risk is not clear. Alcohol probably functions by a "secondary effect," i.e. it adversely affects the ability of the liver to remove estrogen from the blood system, which leads to a rise in blood estrogen levels. As estrogen can stimulate the growth of breast cells, this may raise the risk of breast cancer. Also, breakdown products of alcohol may lead to mutations in cells by affecting proteins that usually protect and repair cellular DNA.

Moderate alcohol intake may protect against cardiovascular disease and it is pertinent to remember that cardiovascular disease is a considerably greater risk to women than breast cancer. Once a patient has developed breast cancer, however, there is evidence that alcohol consumption may not be advisable.

Specific dietary associations with breast cancer

We know that dietary and lifestyle choices may help to prevent breast cancer and its recurrence, and may also prevent the development of other diseases. In recent years, there have been many reports in the press about the role certain foods play in both the development of cancer and protection from it, not all of them substantiated by plausible research studies, so let's explore these in more detail.

Dietary fats

There is some evidence that both the total amount of fat and the amount of saturated fat consumed in the diet are associated with both the risk of developing postmenopausal breast cancer and poorer survival after a breast cancer diagnosis. The sources of such fat are butter, margarine, and cooking oil, as well as

"Alcohol consumption has been linked to an increase in both the risk of developing breast cancer and the likelihood of breast cancer recurrence. Once a patient has developed breast cancer, there is evidence to indicate that alcohol consumption is not advisable."

the fats from meats of various sources and "hidden fats" in cakes, cookies, and snack foods.

Sugars and carbs

In recent years, some studies have suggested that the consumption of carbohydrates has been related to breast cancer risk, however the analysis of all studies performed in this field does not support this and, overall, the conclusion is that there is no association between carbohydrate intake and breast cancer risk.

Dairy products

Despite many misleading media reports, there is no scientific evidence to support the idea that milk or dairy products increase breast cancer risk, or affect prognosis after a breast cancer diagnosis. This misconception stems from the observation that the incidence of breast cancer is low in countries like China where the consumption of dairy foods is low. However, researchers believe that the low incidence is mainly due to other lifestyle differences.

As milk is a complex food that includes vitamins, minerals, carbohydrates, fats, and proteins, dairy-based foods are very difficult to study either in the laboratory or in population studies. Some laboratory studies have suggested that certain proteins in the milk can stimulate cell growth but these results have not been replicated in humans. In contrast, high levels of intake of dairy products have been shown to be associated with a reduced risk of premenopausal breast cancer. As dairy products are an important source of calcium, which is essential for bone health, moderate consumption of low-fat dairy produce is advised.

"There is no evidence to suggest that the consumption of milk or dairy products increases breast cancer risk; the same holds true for meat products. Consuming lean meat in moderation as part of a balanced diet is deemed perfectly safe."

Meat intake

The results of scientific studies concerning the consumption of meat products and poultry are inconsistent and further research is required. Current evidence suggests that the consumption of nonprocessed meat in moderation as a part of a balanced diet is quite safe (see page 18).

Fruit, vegetables, and dietary fiber

Vegetables and fruit may well have a preventative effect against cancer, as they are rich in antioxidants and vitamins, including vitamins C, E, and folate; they are also an important source of dietary fiber.

An antioxidant prevents a chemical process called oxidation in which oxygen molecules are joined with other chemicals to create reactive products. These reactive products have been shown to cause gene damage in cells and such damage may ultimately lead to cancer development.

Despite this clear evidence of protective effects, the evidence for decreased breast cancer risk based on the consumption of fruit and vegetables is limited and further studies are needed. With regard to fiber, studies suggest that a diet rich in dietary fiber is likely to reduce the risk of developing breast cancer.

Phytoestrogens

One of the main foodstuffs consumed in high quantities in Eastern diets is soy. Examples of soy food include beans and cereals, tofu, green vegetables, and soy milk. These foods are enriched in plant chemicals, which have molecules similar to the female sex hormone estrogen and are known as phytoestrogens. They can behave like human estrogen and bind to receptors in cells, preventing naturally occurring estrogen from binding. Because of this property, phytoestrogens are thought to have a protective role against breast cancer by preventing cancer cell growth.

Researchers have tried to establish if consumption of soy and fermented soy (e.g. tofu) is linked to a decreased risk of developing breast cancer, and whether this also relates to reduced breast cancer recurrence rates. There is some evidence to suggest that this is the case, in both Western and Eastern populations.

The picture is somewhat more complicated when a patient has already been diagnosed with breast cancer, as phytoestrogens have the potential to interfere with hormonal treatments which function by binding to the estrogen receptor. There may still be a link between better survival after breast cancer and the consumption of foods containing soy, but further research is needed into this topic.

"Soy-rich foods including edamame beans, dried soybeans, tofu, miso, and soy milk contain phytoestrogens, which have properties similar to the female sex hormone estrogen. These are thought to have a protective effect against breast cancer by preventing cancer cell growth."

Tea and coffee

Green tea, black tea, and coffee are difficult to study as they contain varied ingredients and show batch-to-batch and geographical differences. There have been some animal studies which suggest that green tea extracts may combine with the breast cancer drug Tamoxifen and reduce side effects. Further research is required to confirm these results in humans and also to establish the effects of black tea and coffee in this regard.

Taking the above into consideration, we have prepared a guide to foods to eat more of, foods to eat in moderation and foods you should be cautious of. This is followed by a collection of recipes, which have been carefully devised, incorporating the current evidence to help you toward a healthy, well-balanced diet.

Moving towards a healthier diet and lifestyle

Diet and its effect on health is a complex subject. However limited an individual's diet may be, it will still involve a range of foods, which means a diverse intake of ingredients and nutrients at almost every single meal. From time to time, research studies may identify a potentially protective or causal relationship between a food or nutrient and a breast cancer outcome. There are often reports in the press suggesting that a specific food, food group, or nutrient may increase or reduce your risk of cancer, but it is never that straightforward. It is more often the complex combination of several causal or protective factors that explains the outcome.

Understandably, anyone diagnosed with breast cancer is likely to react to media reports linking breast cancer to the intake of specific foods, but we need to be cautious about interpreting these reports and implementing dietary changes. In particular, cutting out specific foods can be detrimental if it leads to a deficiency of important nutrients. All too often we come across contradictory media reports presenting conflicting advice, just a few months apart.

We know that breast cancer and many other chronic diseases can be slowed and/or prevented by dietary and lifestyle modifications, but it is all about adopting and maintaining a healthy, balanced approach. The following advice is based on this premise:

Balance your diet Nutrition is vital for every cellular process in our bodies. Aim to eat a wide variety of food to ensure you are getting all the nutrients you need. Think about the ingredients you are choosing, and how they will influence your mood and health.

Stay in shape Reaching and maintaining a healthy weight is one of the most important goals for all. Evidence clearly highlights its importance as a means of preventing cancer and the progression of the disease.

Move more Exercise not only mitigates cancer risk through weight reduction, it can also lower levels of estrogen in our bodies and modify the ways in which we physically store and process the foods we eat.

Enjoy your food Think about what you are going to eat, shop wisely (especially for fresh items), take the time to prepare your meals and, above all, enjoy what you eat.

Foods to eat more of ...

These are foods that can offer significant health benefits, so it is worth looking to ensure you include them in your diet on a regular and, in most cases, frequent basis.

Fruit and veg Aim to include at least 5 portions (400 g) from as diverse a range of produce as possible. Particularly good choices include the following:

- **Tomatoes** A powerful source of the antioxidant lycopene (particularly following cooking/processing), which gives tomatoes their redness and has the potential to inhibit breast cancer by stopping cancer cell growth.

- **Cruciferous veg** This food group, which includes broccoli, Brussels sprouts, cauliflower, kale, and cabbage, is an excellent source of phytonutrients, which can help to prevent the formation of cancer cells and stop the spread of cancer.

- **Dark green leafy veg** Vibrant vegetables such as spinach, kale, and beet leaves are loaded with folate, a B vitamin that strengthens your DNA and which can reduce cancer risk.

Wholegrain starchy staples Choose nutrient-rich quinoa, bulgur, spelt, brown rice, potatoes, and wholegrain breads over their refined equivalents.

Beans These are an excellent source of vegetable protein. Vital for growth and development, protein is necessary to enable your body to repair any damage imposed by cancer treatments. In addition to protein, beans provide a range of other valuable nutrients, including calcium, iron, and B vitamins.

Omega-3 rich oily fish Include fish such as salmon, sardines, and mackerel in your diet once or twice each week to ensure you are getting omega-3 fatty acids. Apart from helping to decrease inflammation in the body, these foods can also provide a dietary source of vitamin D to promote calcium uptake by the bones.

Olive oil Make this your first choice for cooking and salad dressings. It is loaded with risk-reducing antioxidants and phytonutrients, and has a higher than typical monounsaturated fat content, which can prevent oxidation, the process which produces free radicals known to increase cancer risk.

Foods to eat in moderation …

Labeling any individual food as "bad for you" or "to be avoided" is misleading. The following foods have received a bad press from time to time but they are important sources of vital nutrients and merit inclusion in a balanced diet.

Red meat There have been many conflicting reports about the positive and negative effects of consuming red meat. A high-quality protein food, meat is also a great source of other valuable nutrients, especially B vitamins and minerals—notably zinc, iron, and selenium. The hem-iron red meat provides is especially beneficial, as it is more easily absorbed than iron from plant sources, and can have a positive impact on energy levels.

On the downside, red meat (fattier cuts, in particular) tends to be high in saturated fats. Eaten in moderation, red meat can play an important role in a healthy diet. Our advice would be to choose leaner cuts, trim off excess fat and aim to keep your intake to an average maximum of 70–90 g per day. You can achieve this by having some meat-free days during the week.

Always avoid overcooking meat using a broiler or barbecue, as this can produce heterocyclic amines (HCA) and polycyclic aromatic hydrocarbons (PAH), which may be carcinogenic.

Dairy foods These are great sources of protein and calcium, the mineral that is so vital for bone health. The calcium in dairy foods is more readily absorbed than it is from plant sources, and when consumed in high levels, is associated with greater excretion of dietary fat. Although dairy foods have relatively high levels of saturated fat, nutritional concerns are linked only to situations where their intake contributes to calorie excess (and therefore weight gain). Given that they are such important sources of micronutrients, we would recommend that dairy foods are consumed on a daily basis (unless, of course, you have a lactose intolerance). Look to gain the benefits from low-fat milk, plain yogurt, and low-fat cream cheese and limit your intake of high-fat cheeses, butter, and cream.

Foods to be cautious of …

No single food is known to cause cancer to develop or to recur. Evidence, however, has identified some foods (and nutrients), which should be eaten in small proportions, or completely avoided, to minimize your risk. These include:

Alcohol As explained on page 12 there is a link between alcohol intake and breast cancer. If you have been diagnosed with breast cancer, it is advisable to avoid (or minimize) alcohol.

Trans fatty acids The use of artificial sources of trans fatty acids increases total cholesterol and lowers the "good" (HDL) cholesterol in the body, so they should therefore be avoided. Watch out for sources in:
  · **ready-made cookies, cakes, and pastries** made with partially hydrogenated fats and oils
  · **hard margarines**
  · **meat products** such as burgers, kebabs, pies, and pastries
  · **fat spreads** made using partially hydrogenated oils
  · **savory snacks** such as potato chips.

Candies It is advisable to limit or avoid sources of refined sugar, particularly those that do not offer other useful nutrients, as their intake can be associated with high blood glucose levels and consequently elevated insulin concentrations, a known risk factor for breast cancer development.

Processed meats Some preservatives used in the production of processed meats, including bacon, ham, and hot dogs, are thought (but not proven) to be carcinogenic. Aside from potential carcinogens, these products are generally high in saturated fat and salt, so it makes sense to limit their intake.

Breakfast

Bircher muesli
with apples and blueberries

Serves 4

1½ cups (120 g) jumbo oats

Scant ½ cup (40 g) spelt flakes

⅞ cup (200 ml) sugar-free cloudy apple juice

1½ cups (350 ml) water

7 Tbsp (100 g) plain yogurt

2 sharp dessert apples,
such as Golden Delicious, finely
sliced or coarsely grated

1 cup (100 g) blueberries

A pinch of ground cinnamon

2 Tbsp raw almonds, coarsely
chopped

This traditional Swiss muesli is more like a summer oatmeal than the muesli we are more familiar with. The grains are soaked to release the creaminess of the oats and served with plain yogurt and fresh fruit for a light breakfast.

Tip the oats and spelt flakes into a mixing bowl and pour on the apple juice and water. Cover and let soak in the refrigerator for 2 hours or overnight.

Spoon the soaked oats and spelt into serving bowls and top with the yogurt, apple, blueberries, cinnamon, and chopped almonds.

Muesli with dried fruit, almonds, and sunflower seeds

10 to 12 servings

45 cups (400 g) jumbo oats

1 cup (100 g) spelt flakes

¾ cup (75 g) raw almonds, coarsely chopped

⅓ cup (50 g) sunflower seeds

3½ oz (100 g) dried figs, finely chopped

3½ oz (100 g) dates, pitted and finely chopped

Making your own, delicious muesli couldn't be simpler. Once you try it you will wonder why you ever bought packages from the grocery store.

Preheat the oven to 325°F (160°C). Line 2 medium baking sheets with baking parchment and set aside.

Stir the oats, spelt flakes, almonds, and sunflower seeds together and divide this mixture between the 2 trays, spreading it evenly. Bake for 12 minutes, or until the almonds are very lightly toasted, stirring once halfway through cooking. Remove from the oven and transfer to a big mixing bowl.

Stir through the dried figs, breaking up any large clumps of fruit as you go, and set aside to cool completely before storing in a large jar or plastic container. Enjoy with milk or yogurt for breakfast.

Apple and cinnamon oatmeal

Serves 4

2½ cups (200 g) jumbo oats

2 sharp dessert apples, such as Golden Delicious, peeled and coarsely grated

2½ cups (600 ml) low-fat cow's milk or almond milk

1⅔ cups (400 ml) water

½ tsp ground cinnamon

With its enticing apple and warming spice flavors, this oatmeal will feel like a real treat on an icy morning.

Put all the ingredients into a saucepan and place over medium heat. Cook the oatmeal, stirring regularly, for about 6 to 8 minutes, until the oats are soft and the apple has broken down slightly.

 Dairy foods add value

After treatment for breast cancer, the risk of osteoporosis is increased. Although the hormone estrogen is typically maligned because of its causal role in breast cancer, it also acts to strengthen bone by facilitating the uptake of calcium. As certain cancer treatments lead to a reduction of estrogen levels and/or earlier initiation of menopause, the inclusion of dairy products within our diets has increasing importance. This warming oatmeal offers a sustaining breakfast that's packed with calcium. It also has the added nutritional benefits of fruit and a good proportion of soluble fiber to sustain hunger levels through the morning.

Tropical breakfast salad

Serves 4

2 small, ripe papayas, peeled, seeded, and sliced

1 small pineapple, peeled and sliced

2 passion fruit, halved

4 Tbsp coconut cream

2 Tbsp mint leaves, coarsely chopped if large

For a super speedy and light breakfast, try this lively and indulgent combination. On a particularly hot day, this salad is wonderful served over crushed ice.

Lay the slices of papaya and pineapple out on a serving platter or individual plates and spoon over the passion fruit pulp. Drizzle with the coconut cream, sprinkle over the chopped mint, and serve.

 The most important meal of the day

Ideally, breakfast should provide 20 to 25% of both our recommended fruit and veg intake and our daily requirements for nutrients. Those of us who eat breakfast typically have a more nutritious, balanced diet overall compared to those who skip it. Without it, we can struggle to meet our daily micronutrient requirements and are more likely to resort to unhealthy snacks through the day to compensate. This can have an adverse impact on weight gain—a risk factor for the recurrence of breast cancer.

Boiled egg and nori asparagus soldiers

Serves 4

4 medium eggs, at room temperature

1¼ lb (600 g) asparagus spears

1 tsp sunflower or canola oil

2 tsp sesame seeds

2 tsp low-salt light soy sauce

1 nori sheet, crumbled into flakes

Spears of crunchy asparagus are the perfect healthy soldiers for dipping into a runny yolk. Teaming this combination with soy, sesame seeds, and crushed nori makes it even more delicious.

Preheat the broiler to high.

Bring a pan of water to a boil, then carefully lower the eggs into the water using a slotted spoon. Boil for 4 minutes for a runny yolk, 6 minutes for a semisoft yolk, and up to 9 minutes for a hard-boiled egg.

Meanwhile, snap off the woody ends of the asparagus and toss the spears in the oil, then lay them on a foil-lined baking sheet. Broil for 4 minutes, turning once.

Remove the baking sheet from the broiler and sprinkle the sesame seeds and soy sauce over the asparagus. Broil for another minute to toast the seeds; the asparagus should be burnished but tender with a little bite within.

Remove the eggs from the water with a slotted spoon and remove the tops of the shells with a knife. Place in egg cups. Sprinkle the asparagus soldiers with the nori flakes and dip away.

 Nutrient-rich eggs

Eggs are a good concentrated source of nutrients, providing all of the essential amino acids, all of the vitamins, except vitamin C, several important minerals, and the powerful antioxidant selenium. In the past, negative press reports have linked eggs to high dietary cholesterol intake but it is now understood that the cholesterol we derive from consuming carbohydrate foods has more effect on our blood cholesterol level. Eggs are particularly valuable when your appetite is depleted. Served with asparagus dipping soldiers, they are the complete health-giving small meal to stimulate the appetite.

Home-baked beans on toast

Serves 4

2 tsp olive oil

1 onion, peeled and finely chopped

2 garlic cloves, peeled and crushed

2 tsp smoked paprika

1 tsp thyme leaves

2 Tbsp tomato paste

14-oz (400-g) can tomatoes

14-oz (400-g) can cannellini beans or pinto beans, drained

1 tsp maple syrup

4 slices of bread

4 Tbsp plain yogurt or low-fat crème fraîche

Homemade baked beans are infinitely tastier and more nutritious than their gloopy, sugar-saturated canned equivalent. These silky beans in a smoky tomato sauce are perfect for a hearty breakfast or brunch.

Heat the olive oil in a large saucepan over medium-low heat. Add the onion and fry gently, stirring regularly, for 5 minutes until softened and golden, adding a little water if necessary. Stir in the garlic, smoked paprika, thyme, and tomato paste and fry the mixture, stirring all the time, for another 2 minutes until fragrant.

Meanwhile, blitz the tomatoes in a food processor until fine. Add to the saucepan and simmer for 10 minutes until slightly reduced.

Now add the beans and maple syrup and continue to simmer for 5 minutes. At this point, the sauce should be reduced and thick.

In the meantime, toast the slices of bread.

Serve the beans on the hot toast with a dollop of plain yogurt or crème fraîche.

 Versatile, sustaining pulses

Beans and other pulses are an economical and versatile food that offer a filling vegetarian alternative to meat. Canned pulses are a convenient fast food that can be added to soups and salads, blitzed to make dips or used to extend meat dishes. Relatively low in calories, yet satisfying, they are particularly useful if you have breast cancer, as weight gain is a common consequence of treatment and a key concern—due to its link with the risk of recurrence.

Baked feta eggs
with tomatoes, kale, and dukkah

Serves 4

1 tsp olive oil

2 garlic cloves, peeled and crushed

4 scallions, roughly sliced

3½ oz (100 g) kale, tough central stalk discarded, coarsely chopped and rinsed

7 oz (200 g) chopped tomatoes (fresh or canned)

4 medium eggs

2¼ oz (60 g) light feta cheese

2 tsp dukkah (see right)

This easy-to-prepare, deeply savory concoction makes for an unusual weekend brunch. Dukkah is a tasty Egyptian spiced nut and seed mix—try making your own (see below) and keeping it in a jar to sprinkle over salads and soups.

Preheat the oven to 350°F (180°C). Have a kettle or pan filled with freshly boiled water and a roasting pan ready.

Heat the olive oil in a large frying pan over medium heat. When it is hot, add the garlic and scallions and fry for a couple of minutes, stirring frequently, until softened and golden. Add the kale and fry for a minute, until lightly wilted. Stir in the tomatoes and let bubble for a minute, then remove from the heat.

Spoon the kale mixture into 4 ramekins and make a dip in the center of each. Crack an egg into each hollow, crumble over the feta, and sprinkle with dukkah.

Stand the ramekins in the roasting tray and place in the oven. With the oven door ajar, carefully pour boiled water from the kettle or pan into the roasting pan until it comes halfway up the sides of the ramekins. Close the oven door and bake for 12 to 15 minutes, until the egg whites are set but the yolks are still lovely and runny. Serve immediately.

Dukkah To make your own, lightly toast ½ cup (50 g) almonds, generous ¼ cup (40 g) sesame seeds, and 1 Tbsp each of coriander, cumin, and sesame seeds in a heavy pan until fragrant, then grind to a coarse powder.

Mexican eggs

Serves 2

4 very fresh medium eggs, refrigerated

2¼ oz (60 g) cherry tomatoes, quartered

1 avocado, halved, pitted, peeled, and sliced

Juice of ½ lime

2 Tbsp cilantro leaves, coarsely chopped

A pinch of dried chili flakes (optional)

2 slices of sourdough or other rustic bread

Freshly ground black pepper

This bright and sunny breakfast sings with vibrant flavor. Be sure to seek out avocados at their peak of ripeness—to fully appreciate their creamy flavor.

For the poached eggs, fill a nonstick frying pan with a 1½-inch (4-cm) depth of water and bring to a simmer. Crack the eggs into a small bowl or ramekins and tip them, one at a time, into the water. Let simmer gently for 3 minutes, then carefully remove with a slotted spoon and drain on paper towels.

Meanwhile, in a bowl, toss together the cherry tomatoes, avocado, lime juice, most of the cilantro, and the chili flakes, if using, and set aside.

Toast the bread and place a slice on each warmed plate. Spoon on the avocado mix, then top with the poached eggs, allowing two per person. Sprinkle with the remaining cilantro, a little pepper, and an extra touch of chili, if required.

Quinoa, flax, and chia seed bread

Makes 12 to 14 slices

1¼ cups (150 g) wholewheat all-purpose flour, plus extra to dust

1½ cups (150 g) quinoa flakes

2 Tbsp milled flaxseeds

2 Tbsp chia seeds

2 tsp baking powder

A pinch of mineral salt

2 Tbsp olive oil, plus a little extra to oil

1 medium egg, beaten

About ⅞ cup (200 ml) tepid water

This fairly dense bread, with its slightly cracked crust, may not win any beauty prizes but it is brimming with flavor and nourishment. The slight nuttiness makes it a perfect breakfast loaf—enjoy with almond butter or a little honey.

Preheat the oven to 400°F (200°C). Lightly oil a 1-lb (450-g) loaf pan and dust with a little flour.

Sift the wholewheat flour into a large mixing bowl and add any bran left in the strainer. Stir through the quinoa flakes, flaxseeds, chia seeds, baking powder, and salt and make a well in the center.

Pour the olive oil, egg, and ⅞ cup (200 ml) water into the well and mix to form a fairly firm dough. If it looks a little dry, add another 1 to 2 Tbsp water. Form a rough loaf shape and place in the prepared pan.

Bake for 40 to 45 minutes, until slightly risen and golden. To check that it is cooked, carefully remove the loaf from the pan and tap the underside. If it sounds hollow, it is cooked. Let cool slightly before slicing and serving.

 Seeds: little nutrient powerhouses

Like nuts, seeds have numerous nutritional benefits. Although they have a high fat content, 75 to 80% of their fat is healthy unsaturated fats. An excellent source of omega-3s and omega-6s, they also provide soluble fiber, phytochemicals, and plant sterols, which are deemed to protect against many noncommunicable diseases, including cancer. Adding seeds to bread is a great way of improving the nutritional status of your loaf—as well as its texture.

Banana bread muffins

Makes 12

4 very ripe medium bananas

4 medium eggs, beaten

3½ Tbsp (50 g) unsalted nut butter

4 Tbsp vegetable oil

½ cup (75 g) raisins

½ cup (50 g) ground almonds

1¼ cups (150 g) whole wheat flour

1 tsp baking powder

½ tsp ground cinnamon

These muffins are great to have as an instant standby nutritious breakfast. Ideal for freezing, simply defrost them and warm through briefly to return them to their just-baked glory.

Preheat the oven to 350°F (180°C) and line a 12-hole muffin tray with paper muffin cases.

Put the bananas, eggs, nut butter, oil, and raisins into a food processor and blend for 2 to 3 minutes, until the bananas and raisins have broken down and the mixture is creamy and mousse-like.

Sift the remaining ingredients into a large mixing bowl, adding any bran and almonds left in the strainer, then fold in the wet ingredient mix until just combined.

Using an ice-cream scoop or tablespoon, divide the mixture between the muffin cases. Bake for 15 minutes, or until risen, golden, and a skewer inserted into the center comes out clean. Let cool slightly and serve warm, or at room temperature.

The muffins will keep in an airtight container for up to 3 days.

Oat and spelt soda bread

Makes 16 slices

3½ cups (425 g) whole wheat spelt flour, plus extra to dust

1 tsp baking soda

A pinch of mineral salt

1 cup (75 g) jumbo rolled oats

4 Tbsp sunflower seeds

2 cups (450 g) plain yogurt

1 Tbsp honey

1 Tbsp lemon juice

No kneading or rising—soda bread has to be one of the simplest, and most delicious things to bake. Spelt flour lends a light nuttiness to this traditional Irish loaf.

Preheat the oven to 400°F (200°C) and dust a nonstick baking sheet with flour. Sift the flour, baking soda and salt into a large mixing bowl and add any bran left in the strainer. Stir through the oats and sunflower seeds and make a well in the center.

Mix the yogurt with the honey and lemon juice, pour into the center of the well and quickly stir to form a sticky dough. Using lightly floured hands, carefully bring the dough together into a loose circle and transfer to the prepared baking sheet.

Sprinkle the loaf lightly with flour, then dust a wooden spoon handle with flour and press down into the surface of the dough to make a deep cross. This will ensure even cooking… and supposedly lets the fairies out!

Bake for 45 to 50 minutes, until a golden crust has formed and the bread sounds hollow when tapped on its underside, checking halfway through cooking. If it is already golden at this point, cover loosely with foil for the rest of the cooking time.

Once cooked, transfer the loaf to a wire rack, cover with a clean, damp dish towel, and let cool. Eat soon after baking, or enjoy toasted for up to 2 days. This loaf also freezes well.

Blueberry buckwheat pancakes

Serves 4

1⅔ cups (200 g) buckwheat flour

1 tsp baking powder

¼ tsp ground cinnamon

1 large egg, beaten

generous 1 to 1¼ cups
(250 to 300 ml) low-fat milk or
almond milk

1½ cups (150 g) blueberries

1 Tbsp butter

Buckwheat flour is a fantastic, gluten-free alternative to regular flour and these deliciously simple, fruity pancakes make great use of this light, distinctive flour.

Sift the flour, baking powder, and cinnamon into a mixing bowl and make a well in the center.

Add the beaten egg and gradually stir in generous 1 cup (250 ml) of the milk to make a fairly thick, smooth batter, adding more milk if necessary. Stir in the blueberries.

Heat a nonstick frying pan over a medium heat. Use a wad of paper towels to wipe the pan with a little butter to grease it. Now add 3 or 4 separate heaping Tbsp of batter to the pan. Once bubbles appear on the surface of each pancake and the top is set at the edges, flip over and fry for a minute or so, until the pancakes are golden and the blueberries are juicy.

Keep warm and repeat with the remaining batter, to make about 12 pancakes in total. Serve alone or with a little maple syrup.

5 WAYS WITH *smoothies*

A healthy, easy-to-digest meal in a glass is that much more appealing than a typical breakfast when your appetite is compromised. Packed with vitamins and minerals to help boost your immune system, smoothies are particularly good following treatment with chemotherapy, when you may be more susceptible to infections. Each of these serves 2.

Banana, ginger, yogurt, and lemon
Blend 1 large banana with chopped ¾-inch (2-cm) piece of peeled ginger, 3½ Tbsp (50 g) plain yogurt, 1 Tbsp honey, 1¼ cups (300 ml) milk, and juice of ½ lemon. Pour into glasses.

Avocado, blueberries, spinach, and banana
Put ½ peeled avocado, 1 cup (100 g) blueberries, a large handful of spinach, 1 banana, and the juice of ½ lemon into a blender with 4 Tbsp water and blitz until smooth. Serve over ice.

Raspberry, apple, and watercress
Put 1⅔ cups (200 g) raspberries, 1 peeled, halved and cored apple, and a handful of watercress sprigs in a blender with 4 Tbsp cold water and blitz until smooth. Pour into glasses over ice cubes.

Beet, strawberry, and orange
Juice 1 large raw beet in an electric juicer, or use ⅝ cup (150 ml) beet juice from a carton. Blend the beet juice with ¾ cup (100 g) hulled strawberries and the juice of 2 oranges. Serve chilled.

Pineapple, mint, and coconut milk
Blend 10½ oz (300 g) peeled pineapple flesh, 2 Tbsp mint, ⅝ cup (150 ml) coconut milk, and 2 cups (500 ml) water. Serve over ice.

Soups

Chilled pea soup with mint and lemon

Serves 4

2 tsp olive oil

1 large shallot, peeled and coarsely chopped

4 scallions, roughly sliced

2 garlic cloves, peeled and crushed

4½ cups (1 liter) low-salt vegetable broth

1 lb (500 g) podded fresh or frozen peas

A handful of mint leaves, plus extra to garnish

Finely grated zest and juice of ½ lemon

Freshly ground black pepper

A vibrant, refreshing summery soup that is effortless to prepare. Serve it as an appetizer, or with crusty bread for a light lunch on a hot day.

Heat the olive oil in a large saucepan over medium-low heat. When the oil is hot, add the shallot, scallions, and garlic and fry for 2 to 3 minutes, until beginning to soften.

Pour in the broth and bring to a boil, then lower the heat and simmer for 5 to 6 minutes to soften the shallot and scallions further. Add the peas and mint and cook for another minute, then remove from the heat.

Stir in the lemon zest and juice, then blitz the soup using a blender until smooth.

Pour the soup into a bowl and place over a larger bowl of iced water. Add a couple of lumps of ice to the soup and stir until chilled. Serve seasoned with pepper and garnished with mint.

Asian miso broth with mushrooms

Serves 4

5 cups (1.2 liters) low-salt vegetable broth

2 garlic cloves, peeled and crushed

½-inch (1-cm) piece of fresh ginger, peeled and finely grated

4 Tbsp white miso paste

4¼ oz (125 g) enoki or shiitake mushrooms, sliced if necessary

3½ oz (100 g) collard greens, coarsely sliced

3½ oz (100 g) sugar snap peas, sliced in half

A small handful of cilantro leaves, to serve

This light and soothing soup is ideal when you might be feeling under the weather. A generous pinch of dried chili flakes would be a welcome addition if you want to add an extra kick.

Pour the broth into a large saucepan, add the garlic and ginger, and bring to a simmer over medium heat. Simmer gently for 10 minutes to infuse the flavorings.

Stir in the miso, mushrooms, collards, and sugar snaps. Simmer for 2 minutes and then serve, sprinkled with cilantro.

 Ginger, not just a culinary spice

Links between the *Zingiberaceae* (or botanical ginger family) and medicinal health benefits are renowned. Digestive soothing and antinausea are typically cited as the primary advantages linked to consuming ginger but its benefits extend beyond this. Cancer patients often describe feverish symptoms for example, and ginger can help alleviate the problem.

Butternut squash and peanut soup

Serves 4 to 6

5 cups (1.2 liters) low-salt vegetable broth

¾ cup (80 g) raw, unsalted peanuts or cashews

1 butternut squash (about 2¼ lb/1 kg)

2 tsp low-salt soy sauce

3 scallions, finely sliced

A small handful of cilantro leaves, coarsely chopped

Lime wedges, to serve

Based on a simple Vietnamese home-style recipe, this comforting soup is smooth, creamy and nutty, with a nod to the delicious complexity of Asian flavors. An unusual combination, it is sure to become a favorite.

Bring the broth to a boil in a large saucepan over medium heat. Add the peanuts or cashews and boil for 15 minutes. In the meantime, peel the squash, cut in half, scoop out the seeds, and chop into large chunks.

Add the squash to the pan and simmer for another 12 to 15 minutes, until both the peanuts and squash are tender. Remove from the heat and blitz in a freestanding blender or with a stick blender until smooth and creamy. Season with the soy sauce.

Serve the soup sprinkled with the sliced scallions and cilantro, with lime wedges on the side for squeezing.

Spring vegetable soup with quinoa

Serves 4

2 tsp olive oil

2 leeks, trimmed, well washed, and finely sliced

⅓ cup (60 g) quinoa

4½ cups (1 liter) hot, low-salt vegetable broth

1 zucchini, diced

3½ oz (100 g) asparagus spears

3½ oz (100 g) frozen edamame beans

3½ oz (100 g) kale, coarsely shredded

A handful of basil leaves, coarsely chopped

4 scallions, finely sliced

A squeeze of lemon juice

Quinoa may seem like an unusual addition to soup but it makes for a wholesome and nourishing alternative to pasta or potatoes. This soup is refreshingly light but hearty enough to make for a satisfying meal.

Heat the olive oil in a large saucepan over medium-low heat. When hot, add the leeks and cook, stirring occasionally, for 5 minutes or until softened, adding a little water if necessary if they look a little dry.

Add the quinoa and pour the broth into the pan. Bring to a boil, then lower the heat and simmer for 5 minutes. Stir in the zucchini and continue to cook for another 5 minutes.

Meanwhile, snap off the woody ends of the asparagus and cut the spears into 2 cm lengths. Add to the soup with the edamame beans and kale and simmer for another 2 minutes, then remove from the heat.

Serve the soup sprinkled with the chopped basil, sliced scallions and a squeeze of lemon.

 Quinoa, the complete protein source

Proteins are vital for healthy cell functions so they are particularly important if you are undergoing cancer treatment. Quinoa (pronounced *keen-wa*) is an exceptionally good plant source of protein. Unlike other protein-rich grains and legumes, it contains all nine essential amino acids needed by the body. Originating in Latin America, this ancient grain was a staple food of the Incas. Naturally high in fiber and a gluten-free plant source, quinoa is just as valuable to us today.

Spiced red lentil and tomato soup

Serves 4

2 tsp olive oil

1 small red onion, peeled and minced

2 garlic cloves, peeled and crushed

2 tsp ground cumin

1 tsp smoked paprika

1 tsp ground turmeric

120 g red split lentils

4½ cups (1 liter) low-salt vegetable broth

14 oz (400 g) large tomatoes, coarsely chopped

A small handful of cilantro leaves, coarsely chopped

Lemon wedges, to serve

Lightly spiced and bolstered by hearty red lentils and fresh tomatoes, this soup makes for an equally satisfying lunch or supper.

Heat the olive oil in a large saucepan over medium-low heat. When hot, add the onion, and fry gently for 5 minutes until softened, adding 1 Tbsp or so of water if it starts to look a little dry.

Add the garlic, cumin, paprika, and turmeric and fry for another minute to roast the spices. Stir in the lentils, broth, and chopped tomatoes and bring to a boil, then lower the heat and simmer for 15 to 20 minutes until the lentils have softened.

Serve just as it is, or if you fancy a smooth soup, whiz in a freestanding blender or using a stick blender until smooth.

Serve sprinkled with cilantro, and with lemon wedges on the side for squeezing.

Spices, a cautionary word

Tastebuds are often dulled by cancer treatments and spices can make your food taste more interesting. However, if you experience mouth soreness or ulcers as a consequence of radiation or chemotherapy treatment, you will need to be judicious with spices. For example, capsaicin, found in chile peppers, is likely to aggravate these conditions. Be reactive to how your body accepts spices in foods, and omit them if necessary. You can always pep up flavor with additional herbs and aromatic vegetables.

Parsnip, apple, and ginger soup

Serves 4

2 tsp olive oil

1 small onion, peeled and minced

1-inch (2.5-cm) piece of fresh ginger, peeled and finely grated

1 tsp ground cumin

1 tsp ground turmeric

1 lb (500 g) parsnips (ideally young and small), peeled and roughly chopped

1 medium to large cooking apple (about 7 oz/200 g), peeled, cored and coarsely chopped

4½ cups (1 liter) low-salt vegetable broth

Freshly ground black pepper

Earthy parsnips and sharp-sweet cooking apples are warmed with ginger and delicate spice in this satisfying soup—perfect to have on standby for a bitingly cold day.

Heat the olive oil in a medium saucepan over medium-low heat. When hot, add the onion and ginger and fry gently for 5 minutes until softened, adding a little splash of water if the mixture appears a little dry.

Sprinkle the cumin and turmeric into the pan and fry for a minute to roast the spices and release their aromas.

Add the parsnips and apple, give everything a good stir, and pour over the broth. Bring to a boil, then lower the heat and simmer for 20 minutes, until the parsnips and apple are very tender.

Blitz the soup in a freestanding blender or using a stick blender until smooth and creamy.

Reheat the soup before serving if necessary, sprinkled lightly with black pepper.

Celeriac soup
with arugula and parsley gremolata

Serves 4

2 tsp olive oil

1 onion, peeled and coarsely chopped

2 celery stalks, roughly sliced

1 medium celeriac, peeled and coarsely chopped

5 cups (1.2 liters) low-salt vegetable broth

Freshly ground black pepper

For the gremolata

1 garlic clove

Finely grated zest and juice of ½ lemon

A handful of parsley leaves

A handful of arugula

3 tsp extra virgin olive oil

Sweet and earthy, celeriac makes a lovely, satisfying soup. This one is given a refreshing, zesty kick with a splash of gremolata.

Heat the olive oil in a large saucepan over medium-low heat. When hot, add the onion and celery. Fry gently for about 5 minutes until softened, adding a little water if the veg look a little dry.

Stir in the celeriac and broth and simmer for 20 minutes, until the celeriac is completely soft.

In the meantime, put all of the gremolata ingredients into a food processor and pulse until finely chopped. Add a little water (up to 1 Tbsp) to let down the consistency of the gremolata, if preferred.

Using a freestanding or stick blender, blitz the soup until smooth and creamy. Serve topped with a dollop of gremolata and a sprinkling of pepper.

Roasted cauliflower and garlic soup

Serves 4

1 large cauliflower (about
2 lb/900 g), cut into florets

6 garlic cloves (unpeeled)

1 large onion, peeled and
coarsely sliced

1 tsp caraway seeds

1 tsp thyme leaves

2 tsp olive oil

5 cups (1.2 liters) low-salt
vegetable broth

Finely grated zest of ½ lemon

Freshly ground black pepper

Roasting cauliflower brings out the sweet nuttiness of
this humble vegetable to delicious effect. Here florets
of cauliflower are roasted with garlic cloves, then blitzed
with broth to make a wonderful velvety soup with a real
depth of flavor.

Preheat the oven to 400°F (200°C).

Tip the cauliflower florets into a large bowl and add the garlic and
onion. Sprinkle with the caraway seeds and thyme leaves, trickle
over the olive oil, and toss well to coat the florets.

Spread the cauliflower out on a large baking sheet in one layer
(you may need to use 2 sheets). Roast in the oven for 20 to 25
minutes, turning halfway through, until the vegetables are lightly
burnished and tender.

Take out the garlic cloves and peel away the skins when they are
cool enough to handle. Tip the roasted veg mix into a blender,
add the peeled garlic cloves and broth, and blend until smooth.

Serve topped with a grating of lemon zest and a sprinkling of
black pepper.

Jerusalem artichoke and chestnut soup

Serves 4

1½ lb (750 g) Jerusalem artichokes

Juice of ½ lemon

2 tsp sunflower oil

1 onion, peeled and minced

2 garlic cloves, peeled and crushed

1 Tbsp thyme leaves, coarsely chopped

3½ oz (100 g) vacuum-packed peeled chestnuts

4½ cups (1 liter) low-salt chicken or vegetable broth

Freshly ground black pepper

A small handful of parsley leaves, coarsely chopped, to serve

This wonderfully warming soup is a great one to make over the Christmas holiday—it's an ideal appetizer to precede a traditional Boxing Day cold spread.

Peel and coarsely chop the artichokes, immediately immersing them in a bowl of cold water with the lemon juice added to prevent discoloration.

Heat the oil in a large saucepan over medium-low heat. When hot, add the onion and fry gently for about 5 minutes until softened, adding a little water if necessary, if it looks a little dry. Add the garlic and thyme and fry for another minute.

Drain the artichokes and add them to the pan along with the chestnuts. Give the mixture a good stir and pour in the broth. Bring to a boil, then lower the heat slightly and simmer for 10 to 15 minutes until the artichokes are tender.

Blitz the mixture in a blender until smooth, season with black pepper, and sprinkle with chopped parsley to serve.

 Lemon, an alternative to salt?

A squeeze of lemon can alter the flavor profile of any dish, sweet or savory. Acidity—like saltiness—in our mouths acts as a stimulant for salivation, increasing our desire for a food. Take on board health concerns about the amount of salt we consume and add a squeeze of lemon as you serve food, instead of reaching for the salt mill. Of course, if you are undergoing chemotherapy and experiencing mouth soreness as a consequence, seasoning with lemon juice isn't advisable as it can aggravate the problem.

Seafood soup
with saffron and fennel

Serves 4

2 tsp olive oil

2 shallots, peeled and minced
or sliced

1 inner celery stalk, minced

1 small fennel bulb, minced

2 garlic cloves, peeled and
crushed

A pinch of saffron strands

4½ cups (1 liter) low-salt fish
broth

2 thyme sprigs, leaves picked

2 large tomatoes, quartered,
seeded, and finely diced

8¾ oz (250 g) skinless salmon
fillets, cut into ¾-inch (2-cm)
pieces

6½ oz (180 g) raw tiger shrimp,
deveined

A small handful of parsley leaves,
chopped

Saffron, fennel, and seafood are made for each other.
In this delicious Mediterranean-style soup, the fragrant
subtlety of saffron brings out the delicate aroma of
fennel and the sweetness of the salmon and shrimp.

Heat the olive oil in a large saucepan over medium-low heat. When
hot, add the shallots, celery, and fennel and fry gently, stirring
occasionally, for 8 to 10 minutes until softened, adding a little
water if the mixture seems a little dry.

Add the garlic and fry for another minute, then crumble the saffron
between your fingers and sprinkle directly into the pan. Pour in the
broth, stir in the thyme and tomatoes, and bring to a boil.

Add the salmon pieces to the pan, lower the heat, and simmer for
2 minutes, then stir in the shrimp and simmer for another minute
or two, until they are opaque and pink.

Serve the soup sprinkled with chopped parsley.

Vietnamese chicken soup (pho ga)

Serves 4–6

For the broth

2 onions, peeled and halved

1½-inch (4-cm) piece of fresh ginger, peeled and coarsely sliced

2 cinnamon sticks

1 tsp black peppercorns

3 star anise

1 oven-ready medium chicken (about 3 lb/1.5 kg)

1 carrot, peeled and coarsely chopped

2 celery stalks, coarsely chopped

5 cups (1.5 liters) good quality, low-salt chicken broth (preferably fresh)

To assemble the soup

1 napa cabbage, shredded

1 Tbsp fish sauce

2 tsp maple syrup

6 scallions, sliced

1 cup (100 g) bean sprouts

A handful each of mint, cilantro, and basil leaves

1 red chile, sliced (optional)

To serve

Lime wedges

Fragrant, soothing, and easy on the stomach, this aromatic chicken soup is a great recipe to have in your repertoire and leaves you some leftover chicken for a salad or sandwiches.

Preheat the broiler to high. Lay the onions and ginger out on a broiler tray and broil for 4 to 5 minutes, turning occasionally, until tinged with brown.

Transfer the onion and ginger to a large brothpot or ovenproof Dutch oven (large enough to hold a whole chicken) and add the cinnamon, peppercorns, and star anise.

Place the chicken in the pot and tuck the carrot and celery around it. Pour over the broth and top off with enough water to just cover the chicken. Place over medium heat and bring to a boil.

Turn the heat down slightly and simmer very gently for 50 minutes to 1 hour, or until the chicken is completely cooked through and tender. Remove the chicken from the pot and set aside to cool slightly. Reduce the broth down by boiling if necessary until you have 5 cups (1.2 liters). Strain.

Peel off and discard the skin from the chicken, then remove the meat from the bone and shred into bite-size pieces.

Return the broth to the heat and add the napa cabbage, fish sauce, and maple syrup. Simmer for 1 minute.

Ladle the soup into warm bowls, add a portion of chicken meat to each bowl, then sprinkle over the scallions, bean sprouts, herbs, and chile, if using. Serve with lime wedges for squeezing.

Italian bean soup
with basil and parsley pesto

Serves 4

2 tsp olive oil

1 onion, peeled and chopped

1 carrot, peeled and chopped

3 garlic cloves, peeled
and crushed

2 bay leaves

2 thyme sprigs

1 Tbsp tomato paste

1 zucchini, diced

4½ cups (1 liter) low-salt
vegetable broth

14 oz (400 g) tomatoes,
quartered, seeded, and chopped

14-oz (400-g) can cannellini
beans

7 oz (200 g) savoy cabbage,
shredded

For the pesto

1 garlic clove, peeled

A handful each of basil and
parsley leaves

¼ cup (20 g) finely grated
Parmesan

2 tsp olive oil

4 Tbsp water

This hearty vegetable and bean soup, served topped
with a dollop of easy homemade pesto, is wonderfully
warming and sustaining for a chilly wintry day.

Heat the olive oil in a large saucepan over medium-low heat. When
hot, add the onion and carrot and fry for about 5 minutes until
softened, adding a little water if necessary, to moisten. Add the
garlic and fry for another minute.

Now add the bay leaves, thyme, tomato paste, zucchini, and
broth. Bring to a simmer and cook for 10 minutes, then add the
tomatoes, beans, and cabbage and simmer for another 5 minutes
to soften the cabbage.

To make the pesto, simply put the garlic, herbs, Parmesan, and
olive oil in a food processor and blitz to a thick paste. Drizzle in
the cold water to let the pesto down, and pulse briefly.

Serve the soup topped with a dollop of pesto.

5 WAYS WITH *nuts and seeds*

A sprinkling of nuts and seeds adds flavor and texture to meals and snacks, with a plethora of nutritional benefits. In particular, flavonoids (in the skins on almonds) and phytosterols (concentrated in sesame seeds) help to reduce blood cholesterol levels. Why not add a sprinkling to your breakfast, salad, or soup …

Hemp, flax, and sunflower seed sprinkle
Mix together 4 Tbsp each of shelled hemp seeds, flaxseeds, and sunflower seeds. Stir though 2 tsp ground cinnamon and sprinkle over smoothies, oatmeal, or Bircher muesli (page 23).

Pepper and maple pecans
Toast scant 1 cup (100 g) pecan halves in a frying pan until fragrant, then add ¼ tsp ground black pepper and 2 tsp maple syrup and dry-fry until sticky. Let cool and enjoy as a snack, or sprinkle over salads, or chop up and sprinkle over Parsnip, apple and ginger soup (page 49).

Pine nut, oregano, and tomato mix
Blitz 8 sundried tomatoes (not in oil) with 2 Tbsp pine nuts and 2 tsp dried oregano in a food processor until fairly fine. Delicious sprinkled over salads and soups, such as the Italian bean soup opposite.

Soy baked almonds and sesame seeds
Mix together scant 1 cup (100 g) raw almonds, 2 Tbsp sesame seeds, 1 tsp vegetable oil, and 1 Tbsp low-salt soy sauce. Roast in the oven at 350°F (180°C) for 10 to 15 minutes, let cool slightly, then chop coarsely. Great as a snack or sprinkled over Asian salads, such as Chicken, cashew, and mandarin salad (page 77).

Paprika sunflower seeds
Mix ¾ cup (100 g) sunflower seeds with 1 tsp olive oil and 1 tsp smoked paprika and toast in a pan for a few minutes. Delicious sprinkled over salads, such as Puy lentil and halloumi salad (page 80).

Salads

Fennel and citrus salad

Serves 4

2 fennel bulbs, tough outer layer removed

1½ tsp fennel seeds

2 large oranges

1 large pink grapefruit

3½ oz (100 g) arugula or watercress leaves

Juice of 2 limes

3 tsp olive oil

Freshly ground black pepper

This refreshing, zingy salad, with its contrasting tastes and textures, makes a lovely light lunch served on its own. It also partners oily fish such as mackerel, salmon, or trout beautifully.

Slice the fennel very finely, place in a large bowl, and sprinkle over the fennel seeds.

To prepare the citrus fruits, cut the top and bottom off the oranges and grapefruit to reveal the flesh and then cut the pith and peel away in vertical strips. Now cut either side of the membranes to release the segments, adding them to the fennel as you go.

Once all the segments have been removed, squeeze out the juice from the orange and grapefruit core and membranes over the bowl of fennel and segments. Set aside for 5 minutes to let the fennel soften slightly.

When you are ready to serve the salad, toss through the arugula or watercress. Mix the lime juice and olive oil together and trickle over the salad. Season liberally with pepper and serve.

Edamame bean, pea, and lemon salad

Serves 4

7 oz (200 g) podded fresh or frozen edamame beans

2 cups (200 g) podded fresh or frozen peas

Finely pared zest (in strips) and juice of 1 lemon

4 scallions, finely sliced

A small handful of parsley leaves, coarsely chopped

A small handful of mint leaves, coarsely chopped

¼ cup (40 g) crumbled light feta or sheep's milk cheese

Freshly ground black pepper

Sweet, tender peas and edamame beans marry perfectly with sharp lemon and feta to make a light salad that will go from cutting board to table in minutes.

Bring a medium pan of water to a boil. Add the edamame beans and simmer for 4 minutes. Now add the peas and heat for another minute, then drain and run under cold water to refresh.

Combine the cooled beans and peas with the remaining ingredients and stir to disperse the flavors. Season with pepper to taste and serve immediately.

 Edamame, the super vegetable

These green soybeans are the only vegetable regarded as a complete protein food—as they contain all nine essential amino acids. Edamame are also a good source of vitamins, minerals, fiber, and phytoestrogens, which are thought to inhibit the growth of cancer cells. It is difficult to find fresh edamame but the frozen beans are available all year round. Frozen soon after picking and podding, their nutrient content is well preserved.

Sugar snap pea and quinoa salad with pistachios

Serves 4

Generous 1 cup (200 g) quinoa

2 cups (500 ml) low-salt vegetable broth or water

7 oz (200 g) sugar snap peas, halved lengthwise

4 scallions, finely sliced

A small handful each of chives, parsley and mint leaves, coarsely chopped

⅓ cup (40 g) raw, unsalted pistachios, coarsely chopped

1½ tsp maple syrup

Juice of 1 lemon

1 Tbsp olive oil

A pinch of dried chili flakes (optional)

Crunchy, sweet sugar snaps and pistachios add a vibrancy to mellow quinoa, which can be cooked and stored in the refrigerator the day before for convenience. Don't be concerned if you haven't got all the herbs to hand—a mix of two will be just as delicious.

To cook the quinoa, bring the broth or water to a boil in a medium pan and add the quinoa. Simmer over medium heat for 15 minutes, or until the quinoa has absorbed the water and is tender but still has a little bite to it, adding a little more water if necessary.

Tip the quinoa into a strainer and briefly run under cold water to cool, then set aside.

Put the sliced sugar snaps into a salad bowl and sprinkle over the scallions, herbs, and pistachios.

Whisk together the maple syrup, lemon juice, olive oil, and chili flakes, if using, and pour this dressing over the salad. Add the quinoa, give everything a good mix, and serve.

 Grow your own herbs

Herbs are a complex resource, rich in antioxidant vitamins and minerals. As they are harvested, however, their nutritional value diminishes. So, grow them at home—in pots on a windowsill or patio, if you do not have a garden—and pick them just before adding to dishes for maximum flavour and nutritional value.

Asparagus and white bean salad

Serves 4

14 oz (400 g) asparagus spears

2 tsp olive oil

1 tsp soy sauce

2 shallots, peeled and minced

Juice of 1 lemon

2 14-oz (400-g) cans cannellini beans, drained

2 large tomatoes, quartered, seeded, and coarsely chopped

A handful of parsley leaves, coarsely chopped

2 Tbsp minced chives

Freshly ground black pepper

Crisp-broiled homegrown asparagus and creamy white beans are brought together with a lemony soy dressing for a delightfully simple late-spring lunch.

Preheat the broiler to high.

Snap off the woody ends of the asparagus and cut the spears into roughly 2-inch (5-cm) lengths. Toss the prepared asparagus in 1 tsp of the olive oil and season with the soy sauce and black pepper. Transfer to a foil-lined baking sheet and broil for 5 to 6 minutes until tender and tinged with brown but still crisp within. Set aside to cool slightly.

Meanwhile, stir the shallots with the lemon juice and set aside to mellow the acerbic tang of the shallots.

Combine the cannellini beans and tomatoes in a large bowl and add the lemony shallots. Toss to mix and then add the asparagus and chopped herbs. Toss lightly and serve.

Middle Eastern beet salad with a grapefruit dressing

Serves 4

Finely pared zest (in strips) and juice of 1 pink grapefruit

2 tsp maple syrup

4 medium beet (about 5¼ oz/150 g each)

½ red onion, peeled and finely sliced

Juice of 1 lemon

3½ oz (100 g) radishes, sliced or cut into quarters

A small handful each of dill, basil, cilantro, and parsley leaves

¼ tsp ground sumac

Raw beet springs to life in this salad, which is adapted from a traditional Middle Eastern recipe. It takes a little time to prepare but the earthy and zingy sweet result will have you making this salad time and time again.

First, prepare the dressing: put the grapefruit zest and juice and the maple syrup into a saucepan and bring to a boil over medium heat. Lower the heat and simmer for 5 to 10 minutes, until of a light, syrupy consistency. Pour into a bowl or pitcher and set the dressing aside to cool while you prepare the other ingredients.

Peel and very finely slice the beet, using a mandolin if you have one.

Tip the sliced beet and red onion into a salad bowl and drizzle over the lemon juice. Set aside for 5 minutes so that the lemon juice can soften the beet slightly and mellow the acerbic tang of the onion.

Combine the beet and onion with the radishes and herbs and sprinkle over the sumac. Drizzle over the dressing and serve.

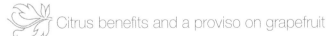 Citrus benefits and a proviso on grapefruit

Citrus fruits are an excellent source of vitamin C, an important antioxidant that helps to boost our immune system. They also contain flavonoids, which may have anticancer properties. You should, however, be aware that grapefruit can interfere with the action of certain drugs, including some used to treat breast cancer. Be advised by your doctor or dietitian as to whether you should avoid this fruit if you are undergoing treatment.

Butternut squash and pearl barley salad

Serves 4

¾ cup (150 g) pearl barley

1 lb (500 g) butternut squash

1 tsp ground cinnamon

1 Tbsp plus 2 tsp olive oil

4 scallions, sliced

A handful of parsley leaves, coarsely chopped

⅓ cup (40 g) raw almonds, coarsely chopped

¼ cup (40 g) crumbled light feta cheese

Juice of 2 lemons

½ tsp ground sumac

Freshly ground black pepper (optional)

This wholesome, delicately spiced fall salad can be eaten warm or cold. The feta adds a salty tang but the salad is also delicious without it, so omit it if preferred.

Preheat the oven to 400°F (200°C).

Bring a large pan of water to a boil. Rinse the pearl barley in a stariner to remove the excess starch, then add to the boiling water and cook for 30 minutes, until tender but not too soft.

Meanwhile, peel and halve the squash, scoop out the seeds, and cut into ⅜ to ¾-inch (1 to 2-cm) chunks. Put into a bowl. Sprinkle with the cinnamon and 1 Tbsp olive oil and toss until the squash is well coated with spice. Transfer to a large roasting pan and roast for 20 to 25 minutes, until tinged with brown and tender.

Check the pearl barley and once it is cooked, drain, rinse briefly with cold water, and drain thoroughly.

Combine the squash and pearl barley in a large salad bowl and sprinkle over the scallions, parsley, almonds, and feta.

Whisk together the remaining 2 tsp olive oil, lemon juice, and sumac and pour over the salad. Toss to combine and finish with a little black pepper, if liked. Either serve straightaway, or let cool before serving.

 Brilliant brassicas

From a nutritional perspective, brassicas such as kale, broccoli, and cauliflower, are impressive. Packed with vital antioxidant vitamins, and minerals, a low-calorie source of protein and an excellent source of fiber, they also contain glucosinolates. Research studies have suggested that these phytonutrients can reduce the risk of developing certain cancers.

Roasted cauliflower salad
with a tahini dressing

Serves 4

1 medium cauliflower, cut into bite-size florets

4 garlic cloves (unpeeled)

2 tsp olive oil

1 small red onion, peeled and cut into wedges

1½ tsp ground cumin

1 tsp ground turmeric

Finely grated zest and juice of 1 lemon

2 Tbsp tahini

4 Tbsp water

3 oz (80 g) baby leaf salad

A small handful of parsley leaves, coarsely chopped

A small handful of cilantro leaves, coarsely chopped

Freshly ground black pepper

With its inviting, spicy flavors, this salad is lovely served warm for lunch. Alternatively, the cauliflower can be roasted the day before—to allow time for the flavors to mingle—and the salad served cold the following day.

Preheat the oven to 400°F (200°C).

Place the cauliflower in a large bowl. Peel and crush two of the garlic cloves and add them to the cauliflower with the olive oil, onion wedges, cumin, turmeric, lemon zest, and half the lemon juice. Season with pepper to taste.

Give everything a good stir so the cauliflower is golden with spice and everything is well dispersed, then tip the mixture into a large baking sheet or roasting pan and tuck the remaining whole garlic cloves in among the vegetables.

Roast in the oven for 20 to 25 minutes until the cauliflower is tinged with brown and tender but still slightly crisp within, turning the florets halfway through cooking. Set aside to cool slightly, picking out and setting aside the whole garlic cloves.

To make the dressing, squeeze the softened roasted garlic out from their skins and mash with a fork. Mix in the tahini, remaining lemon juice, and water until smooth.

Toss the salad greens and herbs together in a large salad bowl, then add the roasted cauliflower mixture. Pour the dressing over the salad. Gently toss everything together to coat in the dressing and serve.

Fattoush salad

½ large cucumber

3 Boston lettuces

4 large tomatoes, quartered, seeded, and sliced

8 radishes, sliced

2 small shallots, peeled and finely sliced

A small handful of mint leaves, coarsely chopped

A small handful of flat-leaf parsley leaves

2 wholemeal pita breads

3 tsp olive oil

2 garlic cloves, peeled and crushed

Juice of 1 lemon

1 tsp ground sumac

This fresh Middle Eastern salad is the perfect way to enjoy some of the finest salad ingredients summer offers: tomatoes, radishes, lettuce, cucumber, and herbs. Tossed in a lemon, garlic, and sumac dressing with toasted pita it's an irresistible combination.

Preheat the broiler to medium.

Halve the cucumber lengthwise, slice, and place in a large salad bowl. Separate the lettuce leaves, tearing larger leaves in half, and add to the bowl. Add the tomatoes, radishes, shallots, and herbs and toss together.

Put the pita breads into a separate bowl. Whisk together the olive oil and garlic. Drizzle half of this mixture over the pitas and turn the pitas to coat well. Lay on a nonstick baking sheet and broil for 2 to 3 minutes until lightly toasted and golden, turning as necessary. Cut into bite-size pieces and set aside.

Whisk the lemon juice and sumac into the remaining oil and garlic mixture and trickle over the salad. Add the toasted pita, toss to mix, and serve.

Watermelon Greek salad

Serves 4

1½ lb (600 g) ripe watermelon

1 cucumber

2 large tomatoes, quartered, seeded, and sliced

½ small red onion, peeled and finely sliced

8 black olives, pitted and quartered

2 tsp olive oil

Juice of 1 lemon

1 tsp dried oregano

A small handful of mint leaves, coarsely chopped if large

½ cup (80 g) crumbled light feta cheese

Naturally sweet, watermelon is a lovely, colorful addition to a classic Greek salad. A breeze to prepare, this wonderfully refreshing salad is just the thing to enjoy for lunch on a hot summer's day.

Cut the watermelon into bite-size chunks, slicing away the thick rind, and place on a large platter.

Halve the cucumber lengthwise and scoop out the seeds, then slice coarsely. Add the cucumber to the watermelon with the tomatoes, red onion, and black olives.

Mix together the olive oil and lemon juice and trickle over the salad, then sprinkle over the oregano, mint, and feta. Give everything a good stir before serving.

 Occasional olives

Olives and olive oil are an integral part of the Mediterranean diet, which is associated with lower incidences of heart disease and cancer. The monounsaturated nature of their fat content does, indeed, give them a healthy profile and they also contain antioxidants and minerals. However, the olives we consume have been cured in salt or brine and are therefore high in sodium. So, while they have a role to play in adding flavor to salads and other dishes, both black and green olives should be consumed in moderation.

Chicken, cashew, and mandarin salad

Serves 4

1¼ lb (560 g) skinless, boneless chicken breast

2 tsp olive oil

2 garlic cloves, peeled and crushed

¾-inch (2-cm) piece of fresh ginger, peeled and grated

½ red onion, peeled and sliced

⅓ cup (40 g) cashews, very coarsely chopped

2 mandarins or clementines

1 cucumber, halved lengthwise and sliced

½ small red cabbage, finely sliced

A small handful of cilantro leaves, coarsely chopped

2 tsp low-salt soy sauce

Juice of 2 limes

This Asian-inspired salad is enticingly bright and flavorsome. It is delicious served warm or cold, as a satisfying lunch or supper.

Preheat the broiler to medium-high. Cut the chicken into strips, about 1 cm thick, and place in a bowl. Add the olive oil, garlic, ginger, red onion, and cashews and toss to mix. Set aside while the broiler heats up.

Transfer the chicken mixture to a foil-lined baking sheet and place under the broiler. Broil for 3 minutes, then turn the chicken pieces, onion, and cashews over and broil for another 3 minutes, or until the chicken is just cooked through. Remove from the broiler and let cool slightly.

In the meantime, finely grate the zest from the mandarins and set aside. Peel the fruit and coarsely chop the flesh.

Put the mandarin pieces in a large bowl with the grated zest, cucumber, cabbage, and cilantro and toss together. Stir through the chicken, cashews, and onion.

Whisk together the soy sauce and lime juice to make a dressing. Trickle over the salad and serve.

Thai beef salad

Serves 4

1¼ lb (560 g) rump steak, ¾ inch (2 cm) thick (about 2 steaks), trimmed of any outer fat

1 tsp vegetable oil

1 cucumber

7 oz (200 g) cherry tomatoes, quartered

A small handful each of basil, mint, and cilantro leaves, coarsely chopped

4 scallions, finely sliced

A handful of ready-to-eat bean sprouts and/or sprouting seeds

2 tsp fish sauce

2 tsp maple syrup

1½ Tbsp lime juice

1 red chile, seeded and minced (optional)

This aromatic and spicy salad is typically laced with sugar but this lighter version uses a little healthier maple syrup instead to complete the authentic combination of sweet, salty, and sour flavors.

Remove the steaks from the refrigerator 15 minutes before cooking. Place a nonstick frying pan over medium-high heat. Pat the steaks dry with paper towels.

Add the oil to the hot pan and when it is really hot, add the steaks. Cook for 1½ minutes each side for rare, 2 minutes each side for medium, and 2¼ minutes each side for well done, turning once only. Remove from the pan and set aside to rest while you prepare the salad.

Halve the cucumber lengthwise and cut across into slices. Place in a large salad bowl with the tomatoes, herbs, scallions, and sprouts. Toss to combine.

Stir together the fish sauce, maple syrup, lime juice, and chile, if using, to make the dressing.

Finely slice the steak, combine with the salad ingredients, and pour over the dressing. Let stand for a few minutes to allow the dressing to soak into the steak, then serve.

Puy lentil and halloumi salad with lemon and garlic

Serves 4

1 cup (200 g) Puy lentils, rinsed

½ red onion, peeled and minced

Finely grated zest and juice of ½ lemon

1 tsp sunflower oil

2 garlic cloves, peeled and crushed

4¼ oz (120 g) light halloumi or provolone, cut into 8 slices

7 oz (200 g) cherry or baby plum tomatoes, halved

3 oz (80 g) arugula leaves

A handful of parsley leaves, coarsely chopped

2 tsp balsamic vinegar

Freshly ground black pepper

Wonderfully savory, halloumi is lovely fried with fragrant lemon zest and garlic and works beautifully with wholesome lentils and sweet tomatoes.

To cook the lentils, bring a large pan of water to a boil, add the lentils, and simmer for 20 to 25 minutes, until tender but not too soft.

Meanwhile, put the onion into a small bowl, add the lemon juice, and set aside while you prepare the remaining ingredients.

Mix together the oil, garlic, lemon zest, and halloumi. Place a large nonstick frying pan over medium heat. When hot, add the halloumi and fry for 1 to 2 minutes on each side until a golden crust has formed, then remove from the heat.

Drain the lentils as soon as they are cooked. While still warm, toss them with the tomatoes, arugula, parsley, and balsamic vinegar. Season with pepper to taste.

Divide the salad between 4 plates. Top each serving with 2 slices of broiled halloumi and serve warm.

5 WAYS WITH *tomatoes*

"A tomato a day keeps inflammation at bay." Lycopene—a potentially powerful carotenoid found in tomatoes— is widely believed to reduce inflammation, which contributes to the development of cancer and several other diseases. Try these lovely, simple ideas for fresh tomatoes.

Slow-roasted tomatoes with garlic and thyme

Place 14 oz (400 g) halved cherry tomatoes on a baking sheet and sprinkle with 4 crushed garlic cloves, 4 tsp thyme leaves, 2 Tbsp olive oil, and a grinding of black pepper. Roast in the oven at 275°F (140°C) for 1¼ hours. Set aside to cool. 4 to 6 servings

Fresh tomato and herb dressing

In a blender or food processor, whiz 10½ oz (300 g) cherry tomatoes with 6 scallions, 2 coarsely chopped garlic cloves, 4 tsp olive oil, the juice of 2 lemons, a good pinch of paprika, and 2 Tbsp coarsely chopped herbs (chervil, parsley, or mint) until smooth. Use to dress your favorite salad. 6 to 8 servings

Broiled cherry tomatoes with balsamic vinegar and garlic

Lay 14 oz (400 g) cherry tomatoes on a baking sheet. Mix together 4 crushed garlic cloves, 1 tsp dried oregano, 2 tsp honey, 4 tsp balsamic vinegar, and 4 tsp olive oil and drizzle over the tomatoes. Broil under high heat for 6 to 8 minutes until tinged with brown. Delicious with broiled steak, tuna, or eggplants. 4 servings

Gazpacho salad

Seed and coarsely chop 6 large tomatoes and mix with 1 minced red onion, 2 coarsely chopped, cored, and seeded red bell peppers, 1 coarsely chopped cucumber, 4 coarsely sliced Boston lettuces, and a large handful of coarsely chopped parsley. Mix together 2 Tbsp olive oil and 4 tsp red wine vinegar and drizzle over the salad. Serve with chunks of wholewheat bread. 4 to 6 servings

Quick tomato salsa

Finely chop 8 large tomatoes and mix with 1 minced red onion, 2 crushed garlic cloves, the juice of 1 lime, and a handful of chopped cilantro. Season with a pinch of dried chili flakes and black pepper to taste. Perfect as a dip for vegetables, with salads or with steamed white fish. 4 servings

Fish
and shellfish

Mussels in a lime, lemongrass, and coconut broth

Serves 4

4½ lb (2 kg) fresh mussels in shells

2 limes

2 lemongrass stalks

1 tsp sunflower oil

2 shallots, peeled and halved

2 garlic cloves, peeled

½ tsp ground turmeric

1⅔ cups (400 ml) can light coconut milk

2 tsp maple syrup

2 tsp fish sauce

10½ oz (300 g) tenderstem broccoli, trimmed

A handful each of cilantro and basil leaves, minced, to finish

This deliciously fragrant and light meal will be ready in minutes. Tenderstem broccoli spears are served on the side to dip into the tasty broth.

Scrub the mussels thoroughly under cold running water and remove the hairy beard from the side of the shell. Discard those with broken shells and any that are open and do not close when sharply tapped.

Cut 1 lime into wedges and set aside for serving. Finely zest the other lime and squeeze the juice. Bruise the lemongrass stalks with the back of a knife, remove the coarse outer layers and finely slice the tender inner part.

Put the oil, shallots, garlic, lemongrass slices, and turmeric into a small food processor bowl or blender and blitz to a rough paste.

Heat a large pot over medium-low heat and add the aromatic paste. Cook, stirring, for 2 minutes, until fragrant. Pour in the coconut milk, maple syrup, and the lime zest and juice and bring to a boil. Lower the heat and simmer gently for 5 minutes, until slightly reduced. Stir through the fish sauce.

Steam the broccoli for 2 to 3 minutes, until just tender; keep warm.

Add the mussels to the broth and cover with a tight-fitting lid. Let the mussels steam for 4 minutes or until they have opened up; discard any that are still closed.

Using a slotted spoon, divide the mussels between 4 large bowls and pour over the broth. Sprinkle over the chopped herbs and serve with lime wedges, with the broccoli spears alongside to dip into the broth.

Broiled mackerel
with soused beet salad

Serves 4

½ red onion, peeled and finely sliced

2 Tbsp cider vinegar

Finely grated zest and juice of 2 limes

4 medium raw beets

1 tsp maple syrup

A pinch of dried chili flakes

1 tsp grated horseradish

8 small mackerel fillets

2 tsp light olive oil

A handful of parsley leaves, chopped

2 Tbsp dill leaves, chopped

A handful of mixed salad greens, such as arugula and watercress

Freshly ground black pepper

Mackerel needs to be paired with something that will cut through its oiliness and this briefly soused beet salad works perfectly. It doesn't take long for the acidity to permeate the beet slices but you can pickle the beet up to 2 days ahead for a more pronounced flavor, adding the herbs and leaves just before serving.

Combine the onion, cider vinegar, and juice of 1 lime in a bowl and set aside to macerate while you prepare the beet.

Peel and slice the beet very finely, ideally using a mandoline. Add the beet slices, maple syrup, chili flakes, and horseradish to the onion mix and stir to combine. Set aside to pickle slightly.

Preheat the broiler to high. Line a broiler pan or baking sheet with foil and place the mackerel fillets, skin side up, on top. Brush the skin with the olive oil and sprinkle with the zest of 1 lime. Broil for 5 minutes, until the flesh on the underside is opaque and flakes when pressed lightly; the skin should be blistered and charred. Squeeze over the juice and sprinkle with the zest of the remaining lime.

To finish the salad, stir through the parsley, dill, and salad greens and season with black pepper. Serve 2 mackerel fillets per person with a portion of the soused beet salad.

 Bold beet

This colorful vegetable is delicious eaten raw, finely sliced, or shredded. Its vivid purple color is attributable to betacyanin, a compound shown in research studies to have anticarcinogenic properties. Beet leaves are usually discarded but they can be used like spinach to gain the benefits of their iron and calcium, as well as vitamins A, C, and E.

Broiled sardines with salsa verde and quinoa salad

Serves 4

12 sardines, cleaned

Generous 1 cup (200 g) quinoa

2 cups (500 ml) low-salt vegetable broth

8 sundried tomatoes (not in oil)

2 scallions, finely sliced

2 red chicory bulbs, finely sliced

3 oz (80 g) arugula leaves

1 tsp olive oil

Freshly ground black pepper

For the salsa verde

½ garlic clove, peeled

1 tbsp capers, drained

2 tsp Dijon mustard

Juice of 1 lemon

A small handful each of parsley, mint, and basil leaves

2 tsp olive oil

3 Tbsp water

Sardines are often overlooked but these small oily fish yield so much flavor. A lively salsa verde and a salad alongside turn them into a delicious meal.

Rinse the sardines inside and out and pat dry; set aside.

Put the quinoa in a saucepan, add the broth, and bring to a simmer over medium heat. Simmer for 15 minutes, until the grains are tender and the broth is absorbed, adding a little water if necessary.

Meanwhile put the sundried tomatoes into a small bowl and pour on hot water from the kettle to just cover. Let rehydrate for 10 minutes, then drain and finely chop the tomatoes.

Transfer the quinoa to a salad bowl and stir through the scallions, chopped sundried tomatoes, chicory, and arugula. Drizzle with the olive oil and season with black pepper.

To make the salsa verde, put the garlic, capers, mustard, lemon juice, herbs, olive oil, and water in a food processor and blitz until fairly smooth but still retaining a slight texture. The sauce should have the consistency of a pesto; if it is a bit thick, let it down with a little extra water. Set aside while you prepare the sardines.

Preheat the broiler to high. Lay the sardines on the rack in the broiler pan and broil for 2 to 3 minutes each side, until blistered and tinged with brown; the flesh should come away easily from the bone. Serve the sardines with the salad and a good dollop of salsa verde.

 Sardines to strengthen bones

A naturally rich source of dietary vitamin D, sardines provide an excellent and sustainable source of omega-3 rich oily fish in our diets. Their vitamin D content can also promote the growth of healthy bones—a key goal following chemotherapy for all cancer patients.

Broiled tuna with cannellini mash and tomato salsa

Serves 4

4 tuna steaks (about 4¼ oz/ 120 g each)

Juice of 1 lemon

1 small red onion, peeled and minced

7 oz (200 g) cherry tomatoes, quartered

A handful of basil, coarsely chopped

3 tsp olive oil

4 scallions, sliced

2 garlic cloves, peeled and crushed

2 14-oz (400-g) cans cannellini beans

½ cup (120 ml) low-salt vegetable broth

A small handful of parsley leaves, coarsely chopped

Freshly ground black pepper

A couple of cans of cannellini beans are a great standby to have in your pantry. They mash beautifully to a creamy textured mash that pairs really well with robust tuna steaks. A quick, zesty salsa brings freshness to this light and satisfying dish.

Have the tuna steaks ready to cook, at room temperature.

To make the salsa, pour half of the lemon juice into a bowl and stir in the red onion. Add the cherry tomatoes and basil and season with black pepper to taste. Set aside while you prepare the mash and tuna.

For the mash, heat 2 tsp of the olive oil in a large saucepan over medium-low heat. When hot, add the scallions and garlic and fry gently for 2 to 3 minutes, until softened and golden.

Drain the cannellini beans and add them to the pan. Take off the heat and mash until the beans have broken down to a chunky texture. Pour in the broth and return to the heat for a minute or so to warm through—the mash should be thick and creamy. Add the chopped parsley and the remaining lemon juice and season with pepper to taste. Keep warm.

Heat a nonstick frying pan over high heat and add the remaining 1 tsp olive oil. When the oil is hot, add the tuna steaks and fry for 2 minutes each side, depending on thickness, turning them once only. The tuna should be pink in the middle.

Remove the tuna steaks from the pan to a warm plate and set aside to rest for a few minutes before serving, with the mash and tomato salsa.

Asian sea bass en papillotte with stir-fried greens

Serves 4

4 sea bass fillets (about 4 oz/ 110 g each)

3 scallions, finely sliced

¾-inch (2-cm) piece of fresh ginger, peeled, finely sliced and cut into fine strips

3 garlic cloves, peeled and finely sliced

1 red chile, finely sliced, with seeds (optional)

5 tsp low-salt light soy sauce

1 tsp toasted sesame oil

1½ tsp sunflower oil

10½ oz (300 g) tenderstem broccoli, trimmed

4 Tbsp water

1 head of collard greens, coarsely sliced

2 Tbsp cilantro leaves, coarsely torn

This dish couldn't be simpler to prepare. Sea bass fillets and aromatics are steamed in little parchment (or foil) tents to condense their delicate flavors and then served with crunchy stir-fried greens.

Preheat the oven to 400°F (200°C).

Lay 4 pieces of baking parchment (or foil), each large enough to loosely encase a sea bass fillet, on a counter. Place a sea bass fillet in the center of each and sprinkle the scallions, ginger, one of the sliced garlic cloves, the chile, 2 tsp of the soy sauce, and the sesame oil evenly over the fish.

Bring the edges of the parchment (or foil) up over the fish and fold the edges together well to seal. Transfer to a large baking sheet. Bake for 10 to 12 minutes until the fish is opaque and flakes easily.

Meanwhile, heat the sunflower oil in a frying pan over low heat. When it just starts to warm up, add the remaining garlic slices and fry very gently until golden and crisp. Remove the garlic from the pan with a slotted spoon and drain on paper towels; set aside.

Place the pan with the garlicky oil back on the stove, over medium heat. Add the broccoli and water and steam-fry for 4 minutes, until beginning soften. Add the greens and continue to stir-fry for 2 to 3 minutes until bright green and tender. Stir through the remaining soy sauce.

To serve, carefully unwrap the parcels, retaining all the juices, and sprinkle the torn cilantro over the fish. Sprinkle the fried garlic over the greens and serve with the fish.

Lemon and almond trout
with new potatoes and sea beans

Serves 4

4 rainbow trout (about 14 oz/ 400 g each), cleaned

14 oz (400 g) baby new potatoes, larger ones halved

4 garlic cloves (unpeeled), bashed

3 tsp olive oil

1 lemon, cut into 8 slices

2 Tbsp parsley leaves, chopped

1 Tbsp tarragon leaves, chopped

2 Tbsp slivered almonds

5¼ oz (150 g) sea beans, well rinsed

Freshly ground black pepper

This lovely, delicate dish is easy enough to prepare as a midweek dinner yet special enough to serve if you are entertaining.

Preheat the oven to 400°F (200°C). Rinse the trout inside and out and pat dry; set aside.

To prepare the potatoes, place them in a large bowl with the garlic, pour over 2 tsp of the olive oil, and season with black pepper. Toss to mix, then transfer to a nonstick baking sheet. Set aside while you prepare the fish.

Lay the trout on a foil-lined baking sheet and place 2 slices of lemon in the belly of each. Sprinkle 1 Tbsp each of chopped parsley and tarragon evenly over the lemon slices. Brush each trout with a little of the remaining oil and sprinkle over the almonds.

Bake both the potatoes and trout in the oven for 20 to 25 minutes, turning the potatoes halfway through cooking, until the trout flesh flakes easily under your fingers when gently pressed and the potatoes are crisp and tender within.

When the trout and potatoes are almost ready, bring a pan of water to a boil. Add the sea beans and cook for 1 minute, until just tender, then drain.

Sprinkle the remaining parsley and tarragon over the trout and serve with the garlicky potatoes and sea beans.

Cod with zucchini, peppers, and saffron new potatoes

Serves 4

4 cod fillets (about 4½ oz/ 125 g each)

2 tsp olive oil (preferably garlic-flavored)

2 red bell peppers, cored, seeded, and roughly sliced

2 medium zucchini, cut into ⅜-inch (1-cm) thick circles

A pinch of saffron strands

14 oz (400 g) new potatoes, larger ones cut in half

2 tsp balsamic vinegar

2 tsp tender rosemary leaves, minced

Freshly ground black pepper

Salad greens, to serve

It doesn't take many ingredients to make a great meal out of cod—simply roasting chunky fillets with rosemary and vegetables and serving with saffron-infused potatoes makes for a tempting midweek supper.

Have the cod fillets ready to cook, at room temperature. Preheat the oven to 400°F (200°C).

Trickle the olive oil into a roasting pan and add the peppers and zucchini. Toss the vegetables so that they are coated in a thin film of oil, season with black pepper, and roast in the oven for 12 minutes, until starting to brown at the edges.

Bring a pan of water to a boil, then crumble in the saffron and add the potatoes. Boil for 12 to 15 minutes, until tender.

Remove the roasting pan from the oven and nestle the cod fillets in among the vegetables, skin side down. Drizzle with the balsamic vinegar and brush the fish with the pan juices. Sprinkle with the rosemary and return to the oven for 10 to 12 minutes, until the cod is opaque and flakes when pressed gently.

Drain the potatoes once they are cooked and keep warm.

Divide the roasted vegetables between warm serving plates and add a cod fillet and a portion of potatoes to each plate. Serve with a sprinkling of salad greens.

Sea beans, a coastal jewel

This succulent seashore plant is rich in a variety of minerals and vitamins A, B, and C. With a taste that is naturally salty, it is increasingly favoured as a means of seasoning food negating the need for added salt.

Fish pie
with a celeriac rosti topping

Serves 4

1 tsp sunflower oil

1 small onion, peeled and minced

1 large leek, trimmed, well washed and finely sliced

1 tsp thyme or lemon thyme leaves, coarsely chopped

⅞ cup (200 ml) low-salt fish broth

½ cup (100 g) low-fat cream cheese

2 Tbsp cornstarch, mixed with 2 Tbsp water

2 tsp wholegrain mustard

8¾ oz (250 g) salmon fillet, skinned and cut into ¾-inch (2-cm) pieces

5¼ oz (150 g) smoked haddock fillet, skinned and cut into ¾-inch (2-cm) pieces

7 oz (200 g) baby leaf spinach

6½ oz (180 g) raw king shrimp, deveined if necessary

1 Tbsp minced chives

2 Tbsp chopped parsley leaves

7 oz (200 g) peeled celeriac

1 Tbsp (15 g) butter, melted

Freshly ground black pepper

A lighter version of the traditional mash-topped family favorite, this recipe is a breeze to prepare and doesn't compromise on flavor. Serve it with seasonal leafy greens or a crisp green salad.

Preheat the oven to 400°F (200°C).

Heat the oil in a large, nonstick sauté pan over medium-low heat. When hot, add the onion, leek, and thyme and fry for about 5 minutes, until softened, adding a little water during cooking if the mixture seems dry.

Add the broth, cream cheese, and cornstarch mixture to the pan and heat, stirring, until thickened, then stir through the mustard. Now add the salmon and haddock pieces and heat very gently for 2 minutes, stirring occasionally and very carefully—so as not to break the pieces up.

Steam the spinach, or cook in a pan with just the water clinging to the leaves after washing, for 1 to 2 minutes to wilt and then transfer to a sturdy strainer. Press the spinach repeatedly against the strainer to drain off as much water as possible.

When the spinach is fairly dry, pat dry with paper towels and lay evenly over the bottom of a 6½-cup (1.5-liter) baking dish.

Carefully stir the shrimp, chives, and half of the parsley through the fish and spoon on top of the spinach. The sauce will be very thick at this stage but will loosen up as the fish cooks.

Coarsely grate the celeriac and squeeze in your hands to remove as much water as possible. Pat dry with paper towels and stir through the melted butter and remaining parsley. Season with black pepper and spoon evenly over the fish.

Bake for 20 minutes, until bubbling around the edges and the topping is crisp and golden. If the top appears to be coloring too quickly in the oven, cover loosely with foil.

Almond-crusted cod with tomato beans

Serves 4

½ cup (50 g) raw almonds

2 tsp wholegrain mustard

1 Tbsp parsley leaves

1 Tbsp basil leaves

Finely grated zest of 1 lemon

4 cod fillets (about 4¼ oz/
125 g each)

1 egg white, lightly beaten

2 tsp olive oil

10½ oz (300 g) fine green beans,
trimmed

1 garlic clove, peeled and crushed

½ tsp paprika

7 oz (200 g) cherry tomatoes,
halved

2 tsp tomato paste

4 Tbsp water

Freshly ground black pepper

Lemon wedges, to serve

Sweet almonds and vibrant herbs are blitzed together to make a tasty, crunchy topping for mild, chunky cod fillets. Tender green beans in a rich tomato sauce are the perfect complement for this easy-to-prepare supper.

Preheat the oven to 400°F (200°C).

Put the almonds, mustard, parsley, basil, and lemon zest in a small food processor bowl and season with black pepper. Pulse until the almonds have broken down to resemble coarse bread crumbs.

Brush each of the cod fillets with a little egg white and sprinkle the almond mixture on top of them, pressing it down to adhere. Place the cod fillets on a nonstick baking sheet and bake for 10 to 12 minutes, until the topping is crisp and golden and the fish flakes when lightly pressed.

Meanwhile, heat the olive oil in a large sauté pan over medium heat. When hot, add the beans and fry for 2 minutes, then add the garlic, paprika, cherry tomatoes, and tomato paste. Fry, stirring for a minute, until fragrant. Add the water and continue to cook for another 1 to 2 minutes, until the beans are tender but still vibrant green and the tomatoes have broken down.

Serve the baked cod with the tomato beans and lemon wedges for squeezing.

 Garlic, a healthy seasoning

Treatments for cancer have a profound effect on our natural immunity. Recent studies suggest that including garlic in our diets may provide a means of redressing this naturally. Further research is needed to verify this, but garlic is known to possess many other health benefits, including vitamins C and B6, selenium, and other antioxidants, including allicin. In a healthy diet, it is particularly valuable as a flavoring alternative to salt.

Roasted spiced monkfish with tomatoes and chicory

Serves 4

1 lb (500 g) monkfish tail fillet

2 tsp ground cumin

1 tsp ground coriander

1 tsp ground turmeric

1 tsp garam masala

2 tsp vegetable oil

2 chicory bulbs, quartered lengthways

7 oz (200 g) cherry tomatoes

1 garlic clove, peeled and crushed

¾-inch (2-cm) piece of fresh ginger, peeled and finely grated

10½ oz (300 g) asparagus spears

2 tsp tamarind paste

Juice of ½ pink grapefruit

1 Tbsp cilantro leaves

The meaty robustness of monkfish ensures it holds its own when teamed with intense flavors. The sweetness of the fish works brilliantly here with aromatic spices and a rich, tangy dressing.

Preheat the oven to 400°F (200°C). Remove any gray sinew still attached to the monkfish, using a small knife.

In a small bowl, mix together the ground spices. Spoon half of this mixture into a large bowl and stir in the oil. Add the chicory and tomatoes to the bowl and toss to coat them in the oily spices, then transfer to a nonstick roasting tray; save the spicy oil remaining in the bowl. Roast in the oven for 8 minutes.

Meanwhile, add the garlic, ginger, and remaining ground spices to the bowl (used to toss the chicory and tomatoes). Now add the monkfish and rub the spices and aromatics all over the flesh.

Snap off the woody ends of the asparagus spears.

After the 8 minutes' roasting, take the roasting tray from the oven and tuck the monkfish in among the vegetables. Quickly toss the asparagus in any remaining spices and oil in the bowl, add to the tray, and return to the oven.

Roast for 10 minutes, or until the monkfish is cooked through and tender in the center; do not overcook, or the flesh will toughen. Remove from the oven and set aside to rest for a few minutes.

Meanwhile, for the dressing, mix together the tamarind paste, grapefruit juice, and cilantro.

To serve, cut the monkfish into slices and serve on a bed of the vegetables, with the dressing trickled on top.

Coconut fish curry with cauliflower "rice"

Serves 4

1 lb (500 g) cod fillet

2 tsp sunflower oil

1 onion, peeled and minced

¾-inch (2-cm) piece of fresh ginger, peeled and finely grated

1 tsp each of ground coriander, cumin, and turmeric

2 tsp tamarind paste

1⅔ cups (400 ml) canned coconut milk

1 low-salt fish broth cube

A pinch of dried chili flakes (optional)

1 medium cauliflower

A handful of cilantro leaves

Lime wedges, to serve

This gently spiced curry, served with steamed cauliflower blitzed to resemble fluffy rice grains, makes for a lovely, comforting supper.

Cut the cod into 1½-inch (4-cm) chunks and set aside.

Heat the oil in a large, deep frying pan or sauté pan over medium-low heat. When hot, add the onion and fry gently for 5 minutes or until softened, adding a little water if it seems dry. Stir through the ginger and ground spices and fry for 2 minutes, until fragrant.

Stir in the tamarind paste and coconut milk, then crumble in the broth cube and add the chili flakes, if using. Simmer for 5 minutes to reduce slightly.

To make the cauliflower "rice," cut the cauliflower into florets and steam for 2 to 3 minutes, until just tender. Let steam-dry off the heat, then tip into a food processor and pulse to break up into ricelike "grains" (alternatively, you can coarsely grate the cauliflower). Keep warm.

Add the pieces of cod to the curry sauce and simmer gently for 2 minutes, being careful not to break the fish up. The fish is ready when it is opaque and flakes when pressed gently.

Serve the curry and cauliflower "rice" sprinkled with cilantro, with a wedge of lime for squeezing.

Fish tagine with herbed bulgar wheat

Serves 4

1 lb (500 g) firm white fish fillet, such as haddock, pollack, or cod

2 tsp olive oil

1 onion, peeled and minced

2 garlic cloves, peeled and crushed

¾-inch (2-cm) piece of fresh ginger, peeled and finely grated

2 tsp ground cumin

1 tsp ground coriander

1 tsp ground turmeric

A pinch of dried chili flakes (optional)

2 tsp tomato paste

A pinch of saffron strands

2 cups (500 ml) low-salt fish broth

14 oz (400 g) tomatoes, coarsely chopped

Finely grated zest and juice of 2 clementines

⅞ cup (200 g) bulgur wheat

2½ cups (600 ml) water

A small handful each of mint, parsley, and cilantro leaves, coarsely chopped

This gently spiced dish is so easy and quick to prepare. To make it even faster to serve up, you can make the sauce the day before, or well in advance and freeze it; simply defrost, bring up to heat, and add the fish at the last minute.

Cut the white fish into 1½-inch (4-cm) pieces and set aside.

Heat the olive oil in a large sauté pan or ovenproof Dutch oven over medium-low heat. When hot, add the onion and fry gently for about 5 minutes until softened, adding a little water if it seems a bit dry. Add the garlic, ginger, cumin, coriander, turmeric, chili flakes if using, and the tomato paste. Cook for 2 minutes, stirring frequently, until fragrant.

Crumble the saffron strands into the broth and add to the pan, along with the chopped tomatoes and the clementine zest and juice. Simmer for 10 minutes, until slightly reduced.

Meanwhile, tip the bulgar wheat into a separate pan, pour on the water, and bring to a simmer. Lower the heat and simmer for 12 to 15 minutes or until the water has been absorbed and the grains are tender, adding a little more water if necessary during cooking.

Add the chunks of fish to the tagine and simmer very gently for 2 minutes, until opaque and flaking to the touch. Be careful not to break the fish up by stirring.

Toss the chopped herbs through the cooked bulgar wheat and serve with the tagine.

5 WAYS WITH *salmon*

Salmon is a good source of omega-3 fatty acids, which play an important role in health. Thought to reduce inflammation and lower blood pressure, they may also be natural chemopreventive agents that can inhibit or impede cancer. These recipe ideas will tempt you toward the recommended one or two oily fish portions each week. Each serves 4.

Grilled salmon with grilled peaches and ginger

Heat a griddle pan over high heat. Finely grate ¾-inch (2-cm) piece of fresh ginger. Rub 4 salmon fillets and 4 halved peaches with the grated ginger and 2 tsp olive oil. Griddle for 6 minutes until the salmon is just cooked and the peaches are syrupy. Serve with lemon wedges and arugula.

Poached salmon, pea and fava bean salad

Flake 4 poached salmon fillets and toss with 2 cups (200 g) each of blanched peas and fava beans, a handful of arugula, the finely grated zest and juice of 1 lemon, a handful of chopped parsley, and ⅛ cup (20 g) crumbled light feta.

Baked salmon with avocado and radish salad

Brush 4 salmon fillets with 1 tsp olive oil and sprinkle with the grated zest of 1 lime. Bake at 400°F (200°C) for 10 to 12 minutes. Meanwhile, toss 1 sliced avocado with 3½ oz (100 g) sliced radishes, ½ sliced cucumber, and a handful of torn cilantro leaves. Dress with 2 tsp low-salt soy sauce mixed with the juice of 1 lime. Serve the salad with the salmon fillets.

Salmon skewers with a lime and ginger dressing

Cut 4 salmon fillets into chunks and thread onto 8 skewers. Mix 1 Tbsp (15 g) melted butter with ¾-inch (2-cm) finely grated ginger and the juice of 1 lime. Brush the skewers with some of the flavored butter and broil for 6 minutes. Meanwhile, toss 2 grated carrots, ½ sliced red cabbage, and 4 scallions together with juice of 1 lime and handful of torn cilantro. Brush the salmon with the remaining butter and serve with the salad.

Sesame-crusted salmon with bok choy

Mix 2 Tbsp sesame seeds with 2 tsp low-salt soy sauce and 1 tsp honey. Spread evenly over 4 salmon fillets and bake at 400°F (200°C) for 10 to 12 minutes. Serve the salmon with the pan juices spooned over and steamed bok choy on the side.

Poultry and meat

Thai turkey lettuce cups

Serves 4

1 lemongrass stalk

2 tsp sunflower oil

1 lb (500 g) lean ground turkey (breast)

Juice of 1 lime

2 tsp fish sauce

3 tsp maple syrup

A pinch of dried chili flakes (optional)

4 Boston lettuces, leaves separated

3½ oz (100 g) radishes, sliced

4 scallions, finely sliced

A small handful of cilantro leaves, coarsely chopped

Full of vibrant Thai flavors, these protein-packed lettuce cups are perfect for a light, fresh-tasting supper, and they can be prepared in minutes.

Bruise the lemongrass stalk with the flat of a knife, remove the tough outer layers, and finely slice the tender inner part.

Heat half the oil in a large frying pan over medium heat. When hot, add half of the ground turkey, along with the sliced lemongrass. Fry for 4 to 5 minutes until golden brown, breaking up the meat into small pieces with a wooden spoon as you go. Remove from the pan and repeat with the remaining oil and turkey.

In a small bowl, stir together the lime juice, fish sauce, maple syrup, and chili flakes, if using.

Return all the cooked ground meat to the pan, add the lime and fish sauce mixture, and stir to combine. Cook over high heat for 2 to 3 minutes, until the turkey is completely cooked through and the mixture is golden brown and sticky.

Spoon the hot meat into the lettuce leaves (or onto a platter lined with the lettuce so that everyone can help themselves). Sprinkle over the radish slices, scallions, and cilantro and enjoy.

Warm chicken liver salad

Serves 4

3½ oz (100 g) asparagus

3½ oz (100 g) fine green beans, trimmed

2 tsp olive oil

14 oz (400 g) chicken livers, trimmed and patted dry

1 tsp paprika

1 chicory bulb, leaves separated

3½ oz (100 g) cherry tomatoes, halved

A handful of arugula leaves

Juice of 1 lemon, or to taste

Freshly ground black pepper

Tender and flavorsome, chicken livers offer so much more than a base for pâtés and terrines. Teaming them with a little paprika and bittersweet salad ingredients creates a dish that sings with texture and taste.

Snap off the woody ends of the asparagus and cut the spears into ¾ to 1¼-inch (2 to 3-cm) pieces. Cut the green beans in half. Bring a pan of water to a boil. Add the asparagus and beans, bring back to a simmer, and cook for 2 to 3 minutes until just tender. Drain and set aside.

Heat the olive oil in a large, nonstick frying pan. Toss the chicken livers in the paprika and add to the hot pan. Fry for 5 to 7 minutes, turning every so often, until golden but still a little pink within.

Toss the warm chicken livers with the asparagus and beans, chicory, tomatoes, and arugula. Add the lemon juice and season with black pepper to taste. Serve immediately.

 Combating fatigue

Tiredness is a common consequence of cancer treatments and for anyone with rheumatoid arthritis the impact can be worsened by iron-deficiency anemia, which reduces the amount of oxygen that can be carried by the blood. Variety meats, such as liver and kidneys, are a concentrated source of iron, which can alleviate such concerns relatively quickly to enable you to get back on your feet.

Turkey and pearl barley risotto with tarragon

Serves 4

2 tsp olive oil

1 small onion, peeled and finely diced

1 leek, trimmed, well washed and finely sliced

2 garlic cloves, peeled and crushed

8¾ oz (250 g) ground turkey

1 cup (200 g) pearl barley

About 5 cups (1.2 liters) hot low-salt chicken broth

2 thyme sprigs

1⅓ cups (150 g) frozen peas

Finely grated zest of ½ lemon

1 to 2 Tbsp tarragon leaves, coarsely chopped

¼ cup (20 g) finely grated Parmesan (optional)

Freshly ground black pepper

Pearl barley offers a wholesome alternative to risotto rice in this soothing, one-pan supper. Tarragon lends a distinctive flavor but you could use thyme or parsley if you prefer.

Heat the olive oil in a large, nonstick sauté pan over medium-low heat. When it is hot, add the onion and leek to the pan and fry gently for about 5 minutes until softened and golden, adding a little splash of water if it seems a bit dry. Add the garlic and fry for another minute.

Now add the ground turkey, turning up the heat slightly. Fry the meat, breaking it up with a wooden spoon, for 2 to 3 minutes until nicely golden. Tip in the pearl barley and fry for another minute.

Pour over 800 ml of the broth, add the thyme, and bring to a boil. Lower the heat and simmer gently for 35 to 40 minutes until the barley is tender, topping off with more broth during cooking if the mixture is looking a little dry, and adding the peas for the last minute of cooking.

Remove the pan from the heat and add the grated lemon zest, chopped tarragon, and Parmesan, if using. Season with black pepper and serve.

Pot-roast chicken
with braised lettuce and peas

Serves 4–6

2 tsp olive oil

7 oz (200 g) shallots, peeled and halved if large

2 leeks, trimmed, well washed, and coarsely sliced

4 garlic cloves, peeled and crushed

2 generous thyme sprigs

2 bay leaves

1 oven-ready free-range chicken (about 3 lb/1.5 kg)

1⅔ cups (400 ml) low-salt

chicken broth

4 Boston lettuces, halved lengthwise

3 cups (350 g) frozen petits pois

2 tsp chopped tarragon or chervil

A squeeze of lemon juice

Freshly ground black pepper

It takes very few ingredients to turn a good quality, whole chicken into a tempting meal. This slow-cooked one-pot chicken is simplicity itself—perfect for an effortless light Sunday lunch.

Preheat the oven to 275°F (140°C).

Heat the olive oil a large ovenproof Dutch oven (big enough to comfortably hold the whole chicken) over medium heat. When the oil is hot, add the shallots and leeks and fry gently, turning occasionally, for 5 minutes or until lightly colored and softened. Add the garlic, thyme, and bay leaves and fry for another minute, until fragrant.

Add the whole chicken to the dish and nestle it in among the vegetables, then pour over the broth. Bring to simmering point, then cover the dish tightly with a lid or foil and transfer to the oven. Cook for 1½ hours, basting the chicken with the pan juices occasionally.

Now turn the oven setting up to 375°F (190°C) and uncover the dish. Roast, uncovered, for another 15 minutes, adding the lettuce and petits pois 5 minutes before the end of cooking. By now the chicken should be tender and cooked through with golden skin. The vegetables should be just tender.

Stir in the tarragon or chervil and finish with a squeeze of lemon juice and a sprinkling of black pepper.

Paprika-roast chicken with sweet potatoes and red cabbage slaw

Serves 4

1 oven-ready free-range chicken (about 3 lb/1.5 kg)

1 lemon

2 tsp smoked paprika

2 tsp olive oil

1 tsp honey

2 garlic cloves, peeled and bashed

A few thyme sprigs

1 onion, peeled and cut into thick slices

1¾ lb (800 g) sweet potatoes, scrubbed and cut into wedges

For the red cabbage slaw

½ red cabbage, shredded

4 scallions, sliced

2 carrots, peeled and coarsely grated

4 radishes, finely sliced

2 Tbsp chives, coarsely chopped

2 Tbsp low-fat plain yogurt

Juice of 1 lime

For Sunday lunch with a difference, try this tasty roast chicken with its sweet and smoky flavors. Teamed with roasted sweet potato wedges and red cabbage slaw it's a mouthwatering assembly.

Preheat the oven to 400°F (200°C).

Place the chicken on a board. Squeeze the juice from the lemon and mix with the paprika, olive oil, and honey. Spread half of this mixture over the chicken. Put the lemon shells, garlic cloves, and thyme sprigs into the cavity.

Lay the onion slices over the bottom of a nonstick roasting pan and place the chicken on top. Roast for 20 minutes, then turn the heat down to 350°F (180°C) and roast for another 15 minutes.

Now toss the sweet potato wedges in the remaining paprika mix and place them around the chicken. (If you are short on space, put the potato wedges in a separate roasting pan.) Roast for another 30 to 45 minutes, basting occasionally and turning the sweet potatoes, until the chicken is cooked through and tender.

Meanwhile, to make the slaw, simply toss together the cabbage, scallions, carrots, radishes, and chives together in a bowl. Mix the yogurt with the lime juice and use to dress the slaw.

Remove the chicken from the oven and let rest in a warm place for about 10 minutes before carving; keep the sweet potatoes warm.

Carve the chicken and serve with the sweet potato wedges and red cabbage slaw.

Sesame beef skewers
with stir-fried rainbow vegetables

Serves 4

1¼ lb (560 g) lean round or other steak

2 tsp toasted sesame oil

1-inch (2.5-cm) piece of fresh ginger, peeled and finely grated

3 garlic cloves, peeled and crushed

2 tsp maple syrup

4 tsp low-salt soy sauce

1 tsp sesame seeds

2 carrots

1 red bell pepper, cored, seeded, and sliced

7 oz (200 g) broccoli, cut into bite-size florets

4 scallions, finely sliced

5¼ oz (150 g) sugar snap peas

Lime wedges, to serve

Bright, colorful, and full of aromatic flavors, this combination will liven up the dullest of days.

Cut the steak into 24 cubes and place in a nonmetallic bowl. Spoon over half the sesame oil, 2 crushed garlic cloves, the ginger, maple syrup, soy sauce, and sesame seeds. Stir to combine and set aside for at least 10 minutes, or overnight in the refrigerator.

Using a vegetable peeler, cut the carrots lengthwise into long ribbons and place in a bowl.

Heat the broiler to high. Thread 3 cubes of meat onto each of 8 metal skewers and lay on a broiler tray. Set aside the marinade. Broil for 3 to 4 minutes, turning once, until browned but still pink in the middle.

Meanwhile, heat a wok or nonstick frying pan over medium heat. Add the remaining sesame oil. When hot, add the red pepper and broccoli and stir-fry for 2 minutes. Add the remaining garlic and the scallions and cook for another minute.

Pour in the remaining marinade and toss in the carrot ribbons and sugar snaps. Stir-fry for another minute or two until the vegetables are tender but still crisp. Serve 2 skewers per person with the stir-fried veg and a wedge of lime.

 Sesame seeds for added crunch

These nutrient-packed seeds are used extensively in Middle Eastern and Asian cooking, either plain or toasted, and as sesame oil and tahini paste. An excellent source of minerals, they are also among the most abundant dietary source of plant lignans, which are known to hinder the production and spread of certain tumor cells. Toasted sesame seeds are an effective seasoning and textural contrast for salads and other dishes.

Fragrant braised beef with dates and chickpeas

Serves 4

2 tsp olive oil

1¼ lb (560 g) lean beef stewing steak, cut into 1-inch (2.5-cm) cubes

6 Tbsp water

1 large onion, peeled and coarsely sliced

4 garlic cloves, peeled and crushed

1-inch (2.5-cm) piece of fresh ginger, peeled and grated

1 cinnamon stick

2 tsp ground cumin

A pinch of saffron strands

2¾ cups (650 ml) hot low-salt beef broth

2¾ oz (75 g) Medjool dates, pitted and sliced in half

14-oz (400-g) can chickpeas, drained

1 medium cauliflower

A small handful each of cilantro and parsley leaves, coarsely chopped

Lemon wedges, to serve

A lighter take on a traditional Moroccan tagine, this mildly spiced braise is warming, aromatic and deeply comforting. Served with cauliflower "rice," it's perfect for supper on a chilly winter's evening.

Preheat the oven to 275°F (140°C).

Heat 1 tsp of the olive oil in a large, nonstick frying pan over medium-high heat. When hot, brown the cubes of meat, turning occasionally, for 3 to 4 minutes until well colored all over; you may need to do this in two batches to avoid overcrowding the pan.

Transfer the beef to a Dutch oven (or tagine). Add 3 Tbsp of the water to the frying pan and swirl it around, scraping up any meaty residue. Pour this deglazing liquor into the Dutch oven.

Heat the remaining oil in the frying pan. Once hot, fry the onion slices for 2 to 3 minutes, turning every so often, until golden. Add the garlic, ginger, cinnamon, cumin, and saffron to the pan and fry for another minute or so, until fragrant. Scrape the onion and spice mixture into the Dutch oven, then deglaze the pan again with the remaining 3 Tbsp water.

Pour over the broth, ensuring the meat is just covered, adding a little more if necessary. Stir in the dates, then cover the Dutch oven with a lid and transfer to the oven. Braise for 1 hour, then take out the Dutch oven and stir in the chickpeas. Return to the oven for another 1½ hours or until the meat is tender.

To make the cauliflower "rice," cut the cauliflower into florets, and steam for 2 to 3 minutes, until just tender. Let steam-dry off the heat, then tip into a food processor and pulse to break up into ricelike "grains." (Alternatively, you can coarsely grate the cauliflower.)

Serve the beef with the cauliflower "rice," topped with a sprinkling of cilantro and with lemon wedges on the side.

Harissa lamb with griddled vegetables and a tahini dressing

Serves 4

1 lb (500 g) lamb neck tenderloin, trimmed of any excess fat

1 Tbsp good quality harissa paste, such as Belazu

2 garlic cloves, peeled and crushed

Finely grated zest and juice of 1 lemon

2 zucchini

1 fennel bulb

1 medium eggplant

2 red bell peppers, halved, cored, and seeded

1 to 2 tsp olive oil

2 Tbsp tahini

4 Tbsp water

A small handful of Italian parsley leaves

Tender neck of lamb is inexpensive and perfect for quick cooking. This spicy, Middle Eastern inspired dish is a cinch to prepare and impressive enough to serve if you are entertaining.

Preheat the oven to 400°F (200°C).

Place the lamb neck tenderloin in a nonmetallic bowl and add the harissa, 1 crushed garlic clove, and half of the lemon zest and juice. Toss well to coat the lamb and set aside for 5 minutes—or leave overnight in the refrigerator if you want to prepare ahead.

Cut the zucchini, fennel, and eggplant into ⅜-inch (1-cm) thick slices; cut each of the pepper halves into 4 wedges. Heat a large griddle pan over high heat. While it is heating, brush the vegetable slices with the olive oil.

Once the griddle is smoking hot, add the lamb and griddle, turning occasionally, for 3 to 4 minutes to brown. Transfer the browned lamb to a baking sheet and roast in the oven for 15 minutes for medium pinkness, 20 minutes for well done.

While the lamb is in the oven, griddle the vegetables in batches for 1 to 2 minutes each side, until tender and tinged with brown. Once cooked, lay them out flat on a baking sheet (as piling them up would cause them to steam and overcook).

Whisk together the remaining garlic, lemon zest and juice, the tahini, and water to make a dressing.

When the lamb is cooked, set it aside to rest for up to 10 minutes before slicing and tossing with the griddled vegetables. Serve drizzled with the dressing and sprinkled with chopped parsley.

Pistachio-crusted lamb tenderloins with roasted pepper salad

Serves 4

3 tsp olive oil

1 lb (500 g) lamb neck tenderloin, trimmed of any excess fat

½ cup (50 g) shelled, unroasted and unsalted pistachios

3 Tbsp Italian parsley leaves

1 Tbsp tender rosemary leaves

1 fat garlic clove, peeled

Finely grated zest of ½ lemon

1 red bell pepper, cored, seeded, and sliced

1 green bell pepper, cored, seeded, and sliced

1 yellow bell pepper, cored, seeded, and sliced

½ red onion, peeled and finely sliced

½ tsp caraway seeds

1 Tbsp cider vinegar

Sweet and vibrantly green, pistachios complement this delicate cut of lamb perfectly. Easy to prepare and quick to roast, the crusted lamb is served with a lovely, textured roasted pepper salad.

Preheat the oven to 400°F (200°C).

Heat 1 tsp of the olive oil in a large, nonstick frying pan. When hot, add the lamb neck tenderloin and fry for 3 to 4 minutes, turning occasionally, until golden brown all over. Remove from the pan and set aside on a board to cool slightly.

Meanwhile, tip the pistachios, 1 Tbsp of the parsley, the rosemary, garlic, and lemon zest into a food processor and pulse until the mixture resembles fine bread crumbs.

Divide the pistachio crumb mixture between the lamb fillets and, using your fingers, pack a layer on top of each fillet to create a crust. Place the fillets in a roasting tray and roast in the oven for 15 minutes for medium pinkness, 20 minutes for well done.

While the lamb is cooking, toss the peppers in the remaining olive oil with the onion and caraway seeds and roast on a separate baking sheet in the oven for 10 to 15 minutes, until tinged with brown but still with a crunch.

Let the lamb rest in a warm place for 10 minutes before serving. Toss the roasted peppers with the cider vinegar and remaining parsley. Cut the lamb into slices and serve with the roasted pepper salad.

Lamb's liver with sage and wild mushrooms

Serves 4

1 lb (450 g) lamb's liver, sliced

2 Tbsp all-purpose flour

2 tsp sunflower oil

2 shallots, peeled and finely sliced

2 garlic cloves, peeled and finely sliced

8¾ oz (250 g) wild mushrooms, wiped clean

8 sage leaves, coarsely chopped

Generous 1 cup (250 ml) hot low-salt lamb broth

A splash of Worcestershire sauce

3½ oz (100 g) arugula, spinach, and watercress leaves

Freshly ground black pepper

Lemon wedges, to serve

Golden and crisp on the outside and meltingly tender within, fried lamb's liver is very good when it's properly cooked. Here wild mushrooms and sage bring out the savory earthiness of this often-overlooked cut.

Rinse the lamb's liver in a colander under cold water and pat dry with paper towels. Season the flour generously with pepper and dust the liver with the seasoned flour.

Heat half of the oil in a large, nonstick frying pan over medium heat. When hot, add half of the liver slices to the pan and fry for 3 to 4 minutes, turning occasionally, until well browned. Set the browned liver aside on a plate and repeat with the remaining liver.

Heat the remaining oil in the frying pan. Add the shallots, garlic, mushrooms, and sage leaves and fry for 2 to 3 minutes until golden. Remove from the pan and set aside on a plate.

Pour the broth into the pan and simmer to reduce slightly. Return the liver to the pan and simmer very gently for a minute or two. Return the mushroom mixture to the pan, add the Worcestershire sauce, and toss to combine.

Serve at once, with the salad greens and lemon wedges.

 Sage for hormonal balance

Historically, sage has been used medicinally to alleviate a range of ailments, including digestive problems, menopausal symptoms, and loss of memory. It was even a component of a medicine used to ward off the plague! Rich in phytochemicals and a good source of vital nutrients, including vitamins A, C, and K and several B vitamins, as well as important minerals, it offers health benefits, but a complex interplay of processes is likely to explain such effects. It is thought that sage's phytochemical content may prevent the formation, block the action and/or suppress the development of cancer from carcinogens.

Roasted pork tenderloin with celeriac, edamame beans, and gremolata

Serves 4

3 tsp olive oil

1 medium celeriac, peeled and cut into ⅝-inch (1.5-cm) cubes

1 pork tenderloin, trimmed of excess fat and sinew

1 tsp thyme leaves, coarsely chopped

Finely grated zest and juice of ½ lemon

1 small garlic clove, peeled and crushed

4 Tbsp Italian parsley leaves, minced

A pinch of mineral salt

1 to 2 Tbsp water

7 oz (200 g) frozen edamame beans

Edamame—nutritious young green soybeans—and celeriac team nicely with roasted pork tenderloin, and a zesty gremolata marries the flavors together nicely.

Preheat the oven to 400°F (200°C).

Spoon 1 tsp of the olive oil into a large bowl and tumble in the celeriac. Stir to give it a fine coating of oil and spread out on a baking sheet in a single layer (use two sheets if necessary). Roast in the oven for 10 minutes.

Meanwhile, heat a nonstick frying pan over medium heat and add ½ tsp olive oil. When hot, add the pork tenderloin and fry for 3 to 4 minutes, turning occasionally, until golden brown all over. Remove the pork from the pan.

Take the baking sheet out of the oven and lay the pork tenderloin on top of the celeriac. Sprinkle with the thyme and return to the oven. Roast for another 25 to 30 minutes until cooked through.

While the pork is in the oven, prepare the gremolata. Simply stir together the remaining 1½ tsp olive oil, the lemon zest and juice, garlic, parsley, and salt and mix in 1 to 2 Tbsp water to loosen the consistency to your liking.

Once the pork is cooked, rest in a warm place for 5 minutes or so. Add the edamame beans to a pan of boiling water and simmer for about 3 minutes until tender but still with a slight bite. Drain well.

Slice the pork and serve with the celeriac, beans, and gremolata.

 Less meat, more veg

Combining meat with soy-rich edamame beans is a great way to maximise the nutritional value of a meal. Pork is a good source of protein and iron to combat lethargy, while edamame beans are low in fat and high in protein, fibre and a host of other vitamins and minerals—a real nutritional powerhouse.

Venison and chestnut stew with pearl barley

Serves 4 to 6

2 tsp sunflower or vegetable oil

1 lb (500 g) venison shoulder, diced into 1-inch (2.5-cm) pieces

About 4½ cups (1 liter) low-salt beef broth

1 large onion, peeled and coarsely sliced

7 oz (200 g) carrots, peeled and coarsely chopped

2 garlic cloves, peeled and crushed

½ cup (100 g) pearl barley

1 Tbsp tomato paste

A few thyme sprigs

2 bay leaves

7 oz (200 g) vacuum-packed chestnuts

4¼ oz (125 g) cremini mushrooms, halved

7 oz (200 g) kale, shredded

Juice of ½ lemon

This stew brings together some of the best flavors of the colder months. The rich, gamey flavor of venison is mellowed with winter vegetables and wholesome pearl barley. Bright, lemony kale cuts through the richness.

Preheat the oven to 275°F (140°C).

Heat half of the oil in a large nonstick frying pan over medium heat. When hot, add the pieces of venison and fry until golden brown on all sides; you may need to do this in two batches to avoid overcrowding the pan. Remove the venison from the pan and transfer to a large ovenproof Dutch oven.

Pour a little of the broth into the hot pan and swirl around, scraping up any residue. Pour this deglazing liquor into the Dutch oven. Wipe out the frying pan.

Heat a little more oil in the frying pan and fry the onion and carrots until golden. Transfer the veg to the Dutch oven and deglaze the pan as above, adding the liquor to the Dutch oven. Finish by frying the garlic in the last of the oil and adding it to the Dutch oven.

Add the pearl barley to the Dutch oven and pour on enough of the remaining broth to just cover everything. Stir in the tomato paste and add the thyme and bay leaves. Place over medium heat and bring the stew to a simmer. Lay a damp piece of wax paper directly on the surface, cover with a lid, and cook in the oven for 1 hour.

Take the Dutch oven from the oven and stir in the chestnuts and mushrooms. If the stew is looking a little dry at this stage, add up to generous 1 cup (250 ml) more broth (or water). Return the Dutch oven to the oven for another hour.

By this stage, the stew should be rich and unctuous, with a fairly thick sauce—thin it a little with water if you wish. The venison should be meltingly tender—if it is still a little tough, return to the oven for another 30 minutes.

For the lemony kale, steam the kale for 2 minutes until tender and bright green. Drain well and sprinkle over the lemon juice. Serve with the stew.

5 WAYS WITH *chicken breasts*

A healthy intake of protein is vital when your body is fighting cancer, and chicken is a great source of all the essential amino acids. Take a fresh, new look at chicken dishes to cook. Each of these suggestions serves 4.

Coconut and lime roasted chicken

Toss 4 chicken breasts in ½ cup (120 ml) coconut milk, the grated zest and juice of 2 limes, 2 tsp grated ginger, and 4 crushed garlic cloves. Roast at 400°F (200°C) for 20 to 25 minutes until cooked through. Serve with a salad of torn cilantro, mint, and basil leaves dressed with a squeeze of lime juice.

Pan-fried chicken with sage and prosciutto

Place 4 chicken breasts between 2 sheets of plastic wrap and beat with a rolling pin to flatten to a ⅜ inch (1 cm) thickness. Lay ½ slice of prosciutto on each chicken breast, top with a sage leaf, and secure with a toothpick. Heat 2 tsp olive oil in a nonstick frying pan over medium heat and fry the chicken breasts for 4 to 5 minutes on each side until cooked through. Season with black pepper and a squeeze of lemon juice. This is good with the asparagus and bean salad on page 67.

Lemon, thyme, and pine nut-crusted chicken

Beat 4 chicken breasts between 2 sheets of plastic wrap with a rolling pin to flatten to a ⅜ inch (1 cm) thickness. In a food processor, pulse the grated zest of 2 lemons, 2 crushed garlic cloves, 2 Tbsp pine nuts, 2 tsp thyme leaves, and 1 slice of wholewheat bread until the mixture resembles fine bread crumbs. Stir through 2 tsp olive oil. Sprinkle over the chicken and bake at 400°F (200°C) for 20 to 25 minutes until cooked through. Serve with a tomato salad or the edamame salad on page 65.

Italian chicken grill

Place 4 chicken breasts in a roasting pan with 14 oz (400 g) cherry tomatoes, 2 chopped eggplant, 2 sliced zucchini, 4 crushed garlic cloves, 1 Tbsp chopped oregano, and 1 Tbsp olive oil. Stir, season with pepper, and roast at 400°F (200°C) for 25 to 30 minutes until the chicken is cooked through. Serve with a drizzle of balsamic vinegar and a sprinkling of basil.

Maple-glazed chicken and scallion skewers

Cut 4 chicken breasts into bite-size pieces and toss in a bowl with 4 tsp maple syrup, 1 tsp low-salt soy sauce, and the juice of 1 lime. Marinate in the refrigerator for an hour. Cut 8 scallions into ¾-inch (2-cm) lengths and thread onto skewers, alternating with the chicken. Grill for 10 to 12 minutes, turning frequently, until the chicken is cooked through and golden. Serve with soba noodles and a salad.

Vegetarian

Imam bayildi with tzatziki and spelt flatbreads

Serves 4

For the eggplants

4 medium eggplants

3 tsp olive oil

1 large onion, peeled and chopped

3 garlic cloves, peeled and crushed

½ tsp ground cinnamon

1 tsp ground cumin

1 Tbsp tomato paste

6 large tomatoes, coarsely chopped

1 tsp maple syrup

Juice of 1 lemon

A small handful of parsley, coarsely chopped

Freshly ground black pepper

For the tzatziki

½ cucumber, peeled, seeded, and grated

Scant ⅓ cup (75 g) low-fat Greek yogurt

1 small garlic clove, peeled and crushed

A squeeze of lemon juice, to taste

1 Tbsp minced mint

A pinch of paprika, to serve

For the spelt flatbreads

2 cups (250 g) whole wheat spelt flour

½ tsp dried oregano

A pinch of salt

1 tbsp baking powder

½ to ⅝ cup (120 to 150 ml) warm water

2 tsp olive oil

This classic Turkish dish is warmed with cinnamon and cumin but you can omit these spices if you prefer—it will still be very tasty.

Preheat the oven to 350°F (180°C).

Halve the eggplants lengthwise and score the flesh in a crisscross pattern. Brush with 1 tsp of the olive oil, transfer to a baking sheet, and roast for 20 minutes, until tinged with brown at the edges.

Meanwhile, heat the remaining olive oil in a frying pan over medium heat. Add the onion and fry gently for 5 minutes until softened. Add the garlic, cinnamon, and cumin and fry for another minute, until fragrant. Stir in the tomato paste, chopped tomatoes, and maple syrup and remove from the heat.

Spoon the sauce on top of the eggplants and return to the oven for another 20 minutes until the eggplants are soft and the sauce has reduced. Season with pepper to taste.

Meanwhile, for the tzatziki, put the grated cucumber in a clean dish towel and squeeze out the excess liquid, then transfer to a bowl and stir in the yogurt, garlic, lemon juice, mint, and a little black pepper. Taste for seasoning and set aside.

For the flatbreads, sift the flour, oregano, salt, and baking powder into a large bowl and make a well in the center. Pour in ½ cup (120 ml) warm water and the olive oil and quickly mix to a dough—if it's a bit dry, add a little more water.

Divide the dough into 8 pieces and roll each out on a lightly floured counter until about ¼ inch (5 mm) thick. Heat a large frying pan over high heat and dry-fry the flatbreads for 1 to 2 minutes on each side until slightly risen and charred.

Sprinkle the baked eggplants with the lemon juice and parsley. Sprinkle the tzatziki with a little paprika. Serve the eggplants with the tzatziki and a flatbread or two. Although delicious hot, this dish is traditionally eaten cold, so save any leftovers for lunch the following day.

Ginger tempeh skewers with soba noodle salad

Serves 4

7¾ oz (225 g) package tempeh

2 tsp rice vinegar

2 tsp sesame oil

2 tsp honey

4 tsp low-salt soy sauce

1-inch (2.5-cm) piece of fresh ginger, peeled and grated

2 small zucchini, each cut into 8 slices

8 shiitake mushrooms, halved

5¾ oz (160 g) soba noodles

4 scallions, finely sliced

3½ oz (100 g) radishes (large and/or small, finely sliced

3½ oz (100 g) sugar snap peas, halved

Juice of 1 lime

Tempeh, made from fermented and compressed soybeans, is like tofu's bigger and stronger cousin. It is delicious marinated in a honey and ginger dressing, then broiled with zucchini and mushrooms and served with a simple soba noodle and Asian vegetable salad.

Cut the tempeh into 16 equal-size pieces. For the marinade, put the rice vinegar, sesame oil, honey, soy sauce, and ginger into a ziplock bag and shake to combine. Add the tempeh, seal the bag, and turn a few times to coat the tempeh in the marinade. Leave in the refrigerator for an hour.

While the tempeh is marinating, soak 8 wooden skewers in warm water (to prevent them catching and burning under the broiler).

Preheat the broiler to high. Remove the tempeh pieces from the marinade, setting aside the marinade, and thread onto the wooden skewers, alternating with the zucchini slices and mushrooms so that each skewer has 2 pieces of each.

Brush the tempeh skewers with a little of the marinade and broil for 5 minutes each side until golden and sticky.

Meanwhile, bring a pan of water to a boil. Add the soba noodles, give them a stir to stop them sticking together, and simmer for 6 minutes or according to the package directions. Drain and rinse under cold water to refresh. Drain well.

Toss the noodles in the reserved marinade and add the scallions, radishes, sugar snaps, and lime juice. Serve the tempeh skewers with the noodle salad.

Zucchini, pea, and feta fritters

Serves 4

14 oz (400 g) zucchini

A pinch of salt

⅔ cup (70 g) frozen peas

½ cup (60 g) all-purpose flour

½ tsp baking powder

2 medium eggs, beaten

½ cup (60 g) crumbled light feta

4 scallions, finely sliced

2 tsp minced dill (or chervil)

A pinch of dried chili flakes (optional)

2 tsp sunflower oil

Grated zucchini keeps these fritters deliciously light and fresh-tasting. An arugula salad—dressed with a fresh tomato dressing, or simply a squeeze of lemon —is the perfect complement.

To serve

3½ oz (100 g) arugula leaves

1 quantity Fresh tomato and herb dressing (page 81), optional

1 lemon

Coarsely grate the zucchini and place in a colander set over a bowl. Sprinkle with a good pinch of salt, toss well, and press down hard on the zucchini several times. Set aside to drain for about 30 minutes, then squeeze out the excess water until the zucchini is fairly dry (this will also exude the salt).

Meanwhile, tip the peas into a small, heatproof bowl. Just cover with boiling water and leave for 1 minute, then drain and set aside.

Sift the flour and baking powder into a large bowl and make a well in the center. Add the eggs to the well and beat, gradually drawing in the flour, to create a smooth batter. Stir in the zucchini, peas, feta, scallions, dill, and chili flakes, if using.

Heat a large, nonstick frying pan over medium-high heat and add 1 tsp of the oil. Place 3 or 4 heaping spoonfuls of the zucchini mixture in the pan, spacing them a little apart, and flatten slightly with the back of the spoon. Fry for 2 minutes on each side, until golden and crisp, then transfer to a plate lined with paper towels and keep warm. Repeat with the remaining mixture, adding more oil to the pan and adjusting the heat as necessary.

Dress the arugula leaves with the tomato dressing and serve with the lemon, cut into wedges. Alternatively, just sprinkle the arugula leaves with lemon juice and serve.

Sweet potato and sugar snap curry with fried cauliflower "rice"

Serves 4

1 lemongrass stalk

2 tsp vegetable oil

3 Tbsp red Thai curry paste

2 garlic cloves, peeled and crushed

1-inch (2.5-cm) piece of fresh ginger, peeled and grated

1¼ cups (300 ml) carrot juice or low-salt vegetable broth

1⅔ cups (400 ml) can low-fat coconut milk

1½ lb (600 g) sweet potatoes, peeled and cut into bite-size chunks

1 medium cauliflower

5¼ oz (150 g) cherry tomatoes, halved

1 yellow bell pepper, cored, seeded, and coarsely chopped

7 oz (200 g) sugar snap peas

Finely grated zest and juice of 1 lime

A handful of cilantro leaves, coarsely chopped

This mild Thai-style curry uses carrot juice rather than broth, which lends a touch of sweetness and flavor.

Bruise the lemongrass stalk with the back of a knife, remove the coarse outer layers, and finely slice the tender inner part. Heat 1 tsp of the oil in a large wok over medium heat. Add the curry paste, garlic, ginger, and lemongrass and fry for 2 minutes until fragrant and golden.

Pour in the carrot juice or broth and the coconut milk and stir to combine. Bring to a boil, then add the sweet potatoes. Lower the heat slightly and simmer for 20 minutes until the potatoes have softened.

Meanwhile, cut the cauliflower into florets and pulse in a food processor (or coarsely grate) until it resembles grains of rice. Set aside.

Add the cherry tomatoes and yellow pepper to the curry and simmer for 3 minutes, then add the sugar snaps and cook for another 2 minutes.

While the vegetables are cooking, heat the remaining oil in a large frying pan over medium heat and add the cauliflower "rice." Fry for 5 minutes until it is tender and beginning to turn golden. Sprinkle over the lime zest.

Sprinkle the lime juice and coriander over the curry and serve with the fried cauliflower "rice."

Split pea and coconut dhal
with carrot and cilantro salad

Serves 4

For the dhal

1¼ cups (250 g) yellow split peas
(chana dhal), rinsed well

2 tsp vegetable oil

1 onion, peeled and minced

3 garlic cloves, peeled and
crushed

1-inch (2.5-cm) piece of fresh
ginger, peeled and grated

1 green chile, seeded for less
heat (if preferred) and minced

2 tsp ground cumin

1 tsp ground coriander

1 tsp ground turmeric

4 large tomatoes, roughly
chopped

⅞ cup (200 ml) low-fat coconut
milk

Freshly ground black pepper

For the salad

4 medium carrots

A handful of cilantro leaves,
coarsely chopped

Juice of 1 lime

Rich, creamy, and aromatic, dhal is the ultimate healthy
comfort food. Pairing it with a carrot and cilantro
salad gives you a vibrant, fresh-tasting meal that is
also deeply satisfying.

In a medium pan, bring about 4½ cups (1 liter) of water to a boil
and stir in the split peas. Skim off any scum from the surface and
put the lid on the pan. Simmer over medium heat for 30 minutes,
adding more water if necessary, until the peas are just tender.
Remove from the heat and let cool.

Meanwhile, heat the oil in a large saucepan over medium-low
heat. Add the onion and fry gently for 5 minutes until softened.
Add the garlic, ginger, chile, cumin, coriander, and turmeric and
fry for 2 minutes, stirring regularly, until fragrant.

Add the tomatoes and coconut milk and simmer for 10 to 15
minutes, until thickened and reduced slightly.

Meanwhile for the salad, using a vegetable peeler, cut the carrots
lengthwise into long ribbons and place in a bowl. Add the cilantro
and lime juice and toss to combine.

Spoon the cooked lentils into the sauce, stir to combine, and
season with black pepper to taste. Bring to a boil, stirring, then
remove from the heat.

Serve the dhal with the carrot and cilantro salad alongside.

Saffron and spring vegetable quinoa pilaf

Serves 4

2 tsp olive oil

1 small red onion, peeled and minced

2 leeks, well washed and finely sliced

2 garlic cloves, peeled and crushed

½ tsp ground turmeric

Generous 1 cup (200 g) quinoa

A pinch of saffron strands

3 to 4½ cups (750 ml to 1 liter) hot vegetable broth

7 oz (200 g) asparagus spears

7 oz (200 g) broccoli, cut into florets

2 cups (200 g) petits pois

¼ cup (30 g) dried apricots, coarsely chopped

Finely grated zest and juice of ½ lemon

2 Tbsp mint leaves, coarsely chopped

1 Tbsp coarsely chopped chives

2 Tbsp parsley leaves, chopped

In this pilaf, sweet, tender vegetables and quinoa are warmed by saffron and turmeric and pepped up with fresh herbs and lemon—perfectly capturing the flavors of spring.

Heat the olive oil in a large sauté pan over medium-low heat. Add the onion and leeks and fry gently for about 5 minutes until softened. Add the garlic and turmeric and continue to fry for another 2 minutes, until fragrant.

Add the quinoa to the pan and stir for about a minute to let the grains toast. Crumble the saffron into the broth and pour 3 cups (750 ml) broth into the pan. Bring back to a simmer, then cover and let steam for 8 minutes, until the grains are almost tender and the majority of the broth has been absorbed.

Meanwhile, snap off the woody ends of the asparagus and cut the spears into roughly 1¼-inch (3-cm) lengths. Add to the pan with the broccoli and stir through the quinoa. If the mixture looks at all dry, pour in a little more broth.

Cover and cook gently for another 4 minutes until the vegetables are tender. Add the peas, stir to distribute, and then remove from the heat. Add a little more broth to moisten if necessary.

Stir through the dried apricots, lemon zes, and juice, and the chopped herbs and serve immediately.

Zucchini "pasta" with kale, basil, and sundried tomato pesto

Serves 4

4 medium zucchini

⅓ cup (40 g) raw almonds

1½ oz (40 g)kale, coarsely chopped, tough stalks discarded

1½ oz (40 g) basil leaves, plus a few extra to serve

8 sundried tomatoes (not in oil), rehydrated in warm water for 10 minutes

Juice of 1 lemon

1 tbsp olive oil

3½ oz (100 g) baby plum tomatoes, halved

Freshly ground black pepper

Raw zucchini shredded into strands like spaghetti, is exceptionally good—especially when it is teamed with a punchy basil pesto. This nutrient-packed raw vegetable dish is just as flavorsome as its more familiar pasta-based alternative.

To make the "pasta," shred the zucchini using a julienne peeler to create strands, or a regular vegetable peeler to form ribbons. Set aside in a large bowl.

Put the almonds in a food processor and pulse until they have broken up into smaller pieces. Add the kale, basil, drained tomatoes, and lemon juice and pulse again to create a thick paste. Add the olive oil and blend again. If the mixture is a little thick, add 1 Tbsp or so of cold water.

Stir the pesto through the zucchini "pasta" with the baby plum tomatoes and serve sprinkled with plenty of black pepper and a few extra basil leaves.

 Avoiding wheat?

Try this appealing wheat-free "pasta" dish that's packed with flavor. For anyone with celiac disease, wheat allergy, or gluten sensitivity, food choices are limited, unless you pay over the odds for "gluten-free" alternatives, which are typically higher in fat due to product flavor modifications used to compensate for the removal of gluten. Gluten is found in so many products—bread, cereals, pasta, pizza, and soy sauce, to name but a few. The innovative use of vegetables can help to make a gluten-free diet that much more interesting.

Speedy spelt pizzas

Makes 2 large pizzas (to serve 2 to 4, depending on appetite)

Ideal for a quick midweek supper, these homemade pizzas can be prepared and ready to eat in a matter of minutes. Spelt flour creates a delicious, nutty base and the dough is leavened with baking powder rather than yeast for a fast rise.

For the tomato sauce

1 tsp olive oil

2 shallots, peeled and minced

2 garlic cloves, peeled and crushed

1¼ cups (300 ml) strained tomatoes

2 Tbsp tomato paste

1 tsp dried oregano

For the base

2 cups (250 g) wholewheat spelt flour, plus extra to dust

1 Tbsp baking powder

A pinch of salt

2 tsp olive oil

½ to ⅝ cup (120 to 150 ml) warm water

For the topping

7 oz (200 g) asparagus spears

6 scallions, halved lengthwise

3½ oz (100 g) cherry tomatoes, halved

4¼ oz (120 g) mozzarella, torn into small pieces

A handful of basil leaves

Preheat the oven to 425°F (220°C).

To make the tomato sauce, heat the olive oil in a large frying pan and add the shallots. Fry for 2 to 3 minutes, until softened, then add the garlic and fry for another minute until fragrant and golden. Stir in the strained tomatoes, tomato paste, and oregano and bring back to a boil. Simmer for about 5 minutes until the sauce is of a thick, spreadable consistency. Set aside to cool.

To make the pizza bases, sift the spelt flour, baking powder, and salt into a large bowl and make a well in the center. Pour the olive oil and ½ cup (120 ml) water into the well and quickly mix to make a fairly stiff dough; if it is a little too dry, add an extra 1 to 2 Tbsp water. Divide the dough in half.

Lightly flour 2 baking sheets, about 14 by 10 inches (35 by 25 cm). Place one piece of dough in the center of one of the baking sheets and roll out until the dough reaches the edges of the sheet to form a large, rectangular base. Repeat with the other portion of dough.

Snap off the woody ends of the asparagus and cut the spears in half. Spread the tomato sauce over each pizza base, leaving a 1cm clear margin around the edges. Sprinkle the scallion, asparagus, tomatoes, and mozzarella over the pizzas and bake in the oven for 8 to 10 minutes until the base is crisp and puffed up and the cheese is melted. Serve sprinkled with the basil leaves.

Poached egg on za'atar kale with almond hummus

Serves 2

For the almond hummus

¾ cup (75 g) raw almonds, soaked in water overnight in the refrigerator

1 Tbsp tahini

1 tsp olive oil

1 small garlic clove, peeled

¼ tsp ground cumin

Juice of 1 lemon

2 to 4 Tbsp water

For the eggs

2 very fresh large eggs, chilled

For the kale

¼ tsp dried thyme

½ tsp ground sumac

1 tsp sesame seeds

7 oz (200 g) kale, coarsely chopped, tough stalks discarded

4 sundried tomatoes (not in oil), rehydrated in warm water for 10 minutes, drained and minced

A squeeze of lemon juice

Freshly ground black pepper

This Middle Eastern inspired dish makes a satisfying and flavorsome meal at any time of day. The hummus can be prepared in advance and kept in the refrigerator for up to 3 days—you might like to double the quantity and enjoy the rest as a snack.

To make the hummus, drain the soaked almonds and place in a food processor. Add the tahini, olive oil, garlic, and cumin and process to a coarse paste. Add half of the lemon juice and 2 Tbsp water and blitz again until smooth. Taste the hummus and add a little more lemon juice if required. If the hummus is still too thick, add up to another 2 Tbsp water to let it down. Scoop into a bowl, cover, and refrigerate until ready to serve.

To poach the eggs, fill a nonstick frying pan with a 1½-inch (4-cm) depth of water and bring to a simmer. Crack the eggs into small bowls or ramekins and tip them, one at a time, into the water. Simmer gently for 3 minutes, then remove with a slotted spoon and drain on paper towels.

Meanwhile, heat a large dry frying pan over medium heat and add the dried thyme, sumac, and sesame seeds. Toast until golden and fragrant—about 1 minute. Add the kale with a splash of water and cook for 1 minute, until the kale has wilted. Remove from the heat and stir in the chopped sundried tomatoes and lemon juice.

Serve each portion of kale topped with a poached egg and a good grinding of black pepper, with a dollop of hummus on the side.

Roasted cauliflower with almonds

Serves 4

1 large cauliflower

2 tsp olive oil

2 garlic cloves, peeled and crushed

1 tsp ground cumin

1 tsp smoked paprika

⅓ cup (40 g) raw almonds, coarsely chopped

Juice of 1 lime

A small handful of cilantro leaves, coarsely chopped

If you haven't roasted cauliflower before, prepare for a revelation. A golden char on the edge of a floret brings out the sweet nuttiness of the vegetable, while the aromatics and almonds in this dish add a warming wholesomeness. This dish is great as a side but it can be a complete meal with the addition of herby quinoa and steamed greens, or a simple salad.

Preheat the oven to 400°F (200°C).

Halve the cauliflower vertically and cut each half into ⅜-inch (1-cm) thick slices. Pile into a large bowl and add the olive oil, garlic, cumin, and smoked paprika. Give it a good stir, so the cauliflower slices are evenly coated.

Transfer the cauliflower to a baking sheet or roasting pan, placing the slices in a single layer, and roast for 10 minutes.

Remove from the oven, turn the cauliflower pieces over, and sprinkle over the chopped almonds. Roast for anothr 10 minutes until the cauliflower is charred at the edges and tender. Sprinkle with the lime juice and cilantro and serve.

 Almonds, a naturally healthy choice

Nuts and seeds provide a powerful complex of phytonutrients, unsaturated fats, soluble fiber, and antioxidant vitamins, shown to reduce blood glucose and lower cholesterol levels. Although high-energy ingredients, they are generally consumed in modest amounts and not typically associated with weight gain. As with most foods, natural (unroasted and unsalted) almonds—eaten with their skins intact—provide the greatest benefits as many of the nutrients are concentrated in, or just beneath, the skin.

Okra, eggplant, and tomato stir-fry

Serves 4

2 medium eggplants

8¾ oz (250 g) okra

2 tsp olive oil

2 fat garlic cloves, peeled and finely sliced

1½ Tbsp tomato paste

7 oz (200 g) cherry tomatoes, halved

3 tsp low-salt soy sauce

3 oz (80 g) baby spinach leaves

Lime wedges, to serve

Okra and eggplant are stir-fried with tomatoes and soy until crisp and pillowy—to create a tempting dish with a rich, savory umami flavor. Enjoy as a side dish or as a meal in itself with steamed brown rice.

Halve the eggplants lengthwise, then cut them across into ⅜-inch (1-cm) thick slices. Trim the stalk ends of the okra, then cut the pods in half lengthwise.

Heat half of the olive oil in a large, nonstick frying pan or wok over medium-high heat. When the oil is hot, add the eggplant slices and fry for 1 to 2 minutes on each side, until well browned (you may have to do this in 2 batches to avoid overcrowding the pan). Remove from the pan and set aside.

Fry the okra in the same way, in the remaining oil, for 1 to 2 minutes each side. Add the garlic to the pan and fry for another minute.

Return the eggplant to the pan and add the tomato paste, cherry tomatoes, and soy sauce. Stir-fry for 1 to 2 minutes until the tomatoes begin to break down. Now add the spinach and stir briefly, then remove from the heat.

Divide the stir-fry between warmed bowls and serve straightaway, with lime wedges.

Eat a rainbow of colors

Advice suggests that at least half of every plate we eat should comprise fruit and/or vegetables. Being reactive to the plethora of colors that these ingredients offer will not only provide diversity within the diet, but also an extensive range of nutrients—to create an appetizing, nutritious meal.

Braised chicory and fennel

Serves 4

4 chicory bulbs

2 small fennel bulbs

2 tsp olive oil

2 garlic cloves, peeled and crushed

⅝ cup (150 ml) low-salt chicken broth

2 tsp thyme leaves, coarsely chopped

Juice of ½ lemon

2 Tbsp chopped parsley

Freshly ground black pepper

This simple and delicate dish makes for a wonderful vegetarian side. To enjoy as a main dish, serve with a robust salad, such as the Asparagus and white bean salad on page 67.

Peel away any tired-looking outer leaves from the chicory and cut in half lengthwise. Remove any tough outer layer from the fennel and coarsely cut into wedges lengthwise.

Heat the olive oil in a sauté pan or large frying pan over medium heat. Add the fennel and chicory and fry for 1 to 2 minutes on each side, until golden (you may need to do this in 2 batches to avoid overcrowding the pan). Add the garlic and fry gently for another minute, until fragrant and softened.

Return all the fennel and chicory to the pan (if browned in batches) and pour over the broth. Sprinkle over the thyme and season with a little black pepper. Bring to a simmer, lower the heat, and braise gently, stirring gently occasionally, for 20 to 25 minutes until the veg are meltingly soft at the edges but still firm to the bite within.

Sprinkle with the lemon juice, sprinkle over the chopped parsley, and serve immediately.

5 WAYS WITH *leafy greens*

Consuming more of these vibrant, low-calorie vegetables can reduce the risk of developing stomach, breast, and skin cancers, while also benefiting your cardiovascular and bone health. Beyond steamed spinach and boiled cabbage, there are so many more interesting ways to enjoy them. Here are five targeted recipes to get you started ...

Japanese Swiss chard
Coarsely chop 7 oz (200 g) Swiss chard, including the colorful stems. Boil for 3 minutes, drain, and submerge in ice water. Drain again and toss with 3 tsp low-salt soy sauce. Crumble over a sheet of nori and serve as a snack or appetizer. 4 to 6 servings

Roasted kale with Parmesan
Coarsely chop 7 oz (200 g) kale, discarding the central stalks. Toss in 1 tsp olive oil and 20 g freshly grated Parmesan and transfer to a baking sheet. Bake in the oven at 275°F (140°C) for 20 to 25 minutes until crisp. 3 to 4 servings

Quick spring green soup
Bring 1 liter low-salt vegetable broth to a boil in a pan. Add 1 cup (200 g) finely chopped collard greens, 1 cup (100 g) frozen peas, and 3½ oz (100 g) watercress and cook for 1 minute. Serve sprinkled with ¼ cup (20 g) grated Parmesan, a squeeze of lemon juice, and black pepper. 4 servings

Spinach with garlic, lemon, and walnuts
Heat 1 tsp olive oil in a large frying and add 2 crushed garlic cloves, the finely grated zest of 1 lemon, and generous ⅛ cup (20 g) minced walnuts. Fry for 2 minutes, then add 7 oz (200 g) baby leaf spinach and wilt for 1 minute before serving. 4 servings

Stir-fried savoy cabbage with almonds
Heat 2 tsp olive oil in a large frying pan. When hot, add 1 tsp caraway seeds and a shredded small savoy cabbage. Fry for 2 minutes, then add 3 Tbsp water and steam-fry for another 3 to 4 minutes, until tender. Serve sprinkled with 20 g coarsely chopped raw almonds. 4 servings

Desserts and Treats

Roasted vanilla and orange plums with pistachios

Serves 4

6 ripe plums, halved and pitted

1 vanilla bean, halved lengthwise and seeds scraped

Juice of 2 oranges

2 tsp maple syrup

3 Tbsp water

¼ cup (30 g) pistachios, coarsely chopped

Roasting plums brings out their natural syrupy sweetness. Here orange juice and vanilla form a delectable fragrant syrup that enhances the flavor of the fruit, while a topping of chopped pistachios provides a contrasting crunch.

Preheat the oven to 350°F (180°C).

Place the plums, cut side up, in a baking dish large enough to fit them in one layer.

Stir the vanilla seeds into the orange juice and combine with the maple syrup and water.

Pour the juice mix over the plums, top with the vanilla bean, and sprinkle over the pistachios. Bake in the oven for 25 to 30 minutes, until the plums are tender and syrupy. Serve warm, with a dollop of plain yogurt.

 Satisfying a sweet tooth … naturally

Ripe fruits are naturally sweet and contain a breadth of nutritive benefits, so from an evolutionary perspective we are programmed to enjoy—and gain from—them. Desserts that are naturally rich in nutrient-rich sweetness, which do not call for the addition of cream or a calorie-laden sauce, belong in a healthy diet.

Oaty pear and blackberry crumble

Serves 4 to 6

For the filling

1¾ lb (800 g) ripe pears

2¾ cups (400 g) blackberries

¼ cup (40 g) golden raisins, very coarsely chopped

Juice of ½ lemon

2 tsp maple syrup

For the topping

½ cup (50 g) raw almonds

Generous 1 cup (100 g) rolled oats

1 tsp ground cinnamon

2 tsp maple syrup

2 tsp sunflower oil

This lighter take on a comforting crumble tastes just as good as the original. Ripe pears and blackberries need the minimum of additional sweetness and the granola-like topping lends a welcome crunch.

Preheat the oven to 400°F (200°C).

For the filling, peel, core, and coarsely chop the pears and place them in a medium saucepan with the blackberries, golden raisins, lemon juice, and maple syrup. Cook over medium-low heat, stirring occasionally, for 5 minutes until the fruit is beginning to soften.

Transfer the fruit to a fairly shallow 6½-cup (1.5-liter) baking dish and set aside while you prepare the topping.

For the topping, tip the almonds into a food processor and pulse until broken up into small chunks. Add the oats, cinnamon, maple syrup, and oil and pulse a few more times until the mixture forms small clumps.

Sprinkle the topping evenly over the fruit and bake in the oven for 20 minutes, until the topping is golden and the filling is bubbling around the edges. Check the crumble during cooking—if the top is golden before 20 minutes have elapsed, cover loosely with foil for the rest of the cooking time.

Serve warm, with a spoonful of yogurt or low-fat crème fraîche.

Baked stuffed apples
with cinnamon, dried figs, and raisins

Serves 4

4 dessert apples

Juice of ½ lemon

⅓ cup (50 g) raisins

1¾ oz (50 g) dried figs,
finely chopped

1 tsp maple syrup

1 tsp ground cinnamon

1 tsp butter

4 Tbsp water

Enjoy this classic, fall dessert warm from the oven or cold with some plain yogurt. Easy to prepare, it's a lovely way to enjoy the apple harvest.

Preheat the oven to 350°F (180°C).

Using an apple corer, remove the cores from the apples and make a shallow cut around the circumference of each apple to stop the skin from splitting during cooking.

Stand the apples in a fairly deep baking dish and sprinkle over the lemon juice. Mix the raisins, figs, maple syrup, and cinnamon together and spoon into the apple cavities, filling them to the top. Dot the top of each apple with butter and spoon the water into the bottom of the dish.

Cover the dish with foil and bake for 15 minutes, then remove the foil and bake for another 10 minutes, until the apples have softened and the juices in the dish are syrupy. Serve warm, with a dollop of plain yogurt.

Pineapple and star anise carpaccio

Serves 4 to 6

2 Tbsp maple syrup

1 star anise

Finely grated zest and juice of 1 lime

2 Tbsp water

1 large ripe pineapple

2 Tbsp mint leaves, coarsely chopped

This simple, vibrant dessert is just the thing to enjoy on a warm summer's eve. The anise fragrance from the star anise adds an enticing, warming spice to lively fresh pineapple.

Put the maple syrup, star anise, lime juice, and water in a saucepan and place over medium heat. Simmer for 5 to 10 minutes, until the mixture is of a light syrup consistency. Remove from the heat, discard the star anise, and let cool.

Place the pineapple on a board and cut off the top and bottom. Slice down the sides of the pineapple to remove the skin and then prise out any brown "eyes" that are left.

Turn the pineapple onto its side and slice as thinly as possible. Lay the slices out onto a serving dish and drizzle over the syrup. Sprinkle over the lime zest and mint leaves and serve.

If you are serving the carpaccio on a particularly hot day, lay the pineapple slices over a bed of crushed ice.

 Bromelain

A natural enzyme found in pineapple, bromelain has been linked to the alleviation of symptoms associated with chemotherapy treatment, including inflammation and diarrhea. As with many positive dietary cancer attestations, evidence is not yet conclusive, but inclusion of pineapple in the diet may alleviate joint and gastrointestinal upsets commonly experienced following chemotherapy treatment.

Earl Grey poached pears with warm chocolate sauce

Serves 4

3 Earl Grey tea bags

Scant 3 cups (700 ml) boiling water

4 ripe pears

Juice of ½ lemon

2 Tbsp honey

For the chocolate sauce

3 oz (80 g) semisweet chocolate, minimum 70% cocoa solids

1 tsp vanilla extract

6 Tbsp almond milk

Gently poaching pears with the subtle aromas of Earl Grey tea, instead of the usual alcohol and sugar-spiked liquor, renders them tender and fragrant. Cloaked in a warm chocolate sauce, they are wonderfully indulgent.

Immerse the tea bags in the boiling water and let infuse for 3 minutes, until fragrant. Strain the tea and set aside.

Carefully peel the pears. Using a teaspoon or melon baller, scoop out the core and cut out the woody base from each pear.

Stand the pears in a saucepan in which they fit quite snugly and sprinkle over the lemon juice and honey. Pour over the tea and place the pan over medium-low heat. Bring to a simmer and cook gently, adjusting the heat if necessary, for 25 minutes until the pears are tender right through.

Lift out the pears with a slotted spoon, slice them in half, and place in a bowl; keep warm.

Put the pan back over high heat and let the liquor bubble for 5 to 10 minutes to reduce until syrupy. Set aside.

For the sauce, finely chop the chocolate and put into a heatproof bowl. Place over a pan of just-boiled water, ensuring that the bottom of the bowl is not in direct contact with the water. Let the chocolate melt, stirring occasionally. As soon as it has melted, remove the bowl from the pan. Stir in the vanilla extract and almond milk to make a thick sauce.

Serve 2 pear halves per person, drizzled with the reduced syrup and topped with the warm chocolate sauce.

Chocolate mousse with raspberries

Serves 4

3½ oz (100 g) semisweet chocolate, minimum 70% cocoa solids

7 Tbsp (100 ml) coconut milk

1 very ripe avocado

4 pitted Medjool dates, coarsely chopped

1 tsp vanilla extract

1⅔ cups (200 g) raspberries

This luxurious dessert is the ultimate guilt-free indulgence for anybody wanting to eat more mindfully. The rich creaminess of avocado gives the mousse its silky texture while the fudgy sweetness of dates provides a foil for the tart raspberries.

Finely chop the chocolate and put into a heatproof bowl with the coconut milk. Place over a pan of just-boiled water, ensuring that the bottom of the bowl is not in direct contact with the water. Let the chocolate melt, stirring occasionally.

Once the chocolate has melted, remove the bowl from the pan and set aside to cool for 10 minutes.

Meanwhile, halve the avocado, remove the pit, and scoop the flesh from the skin into a food processor. Add the dates and blend, scraping down the sides occasionally, until smooth and creamy; this should take 2 to 3 minutes.

Scrape the melted chocolate mixture into the food processor, add the vanilla extract, and blend again for a couple of minutes, until smooth. Divide equally between 4 serving dishes. These mousses can be eaten straightaway or chilled for a couple of hours before serving.

When ready to serve, coarsely crush the raspberries in a bowl with the back of a fork. Serve the chocolate mousses topped with the crushed raspberries.

Banana and berry soft-serve ice

Serves 4

2 large, very ripe bananas

1 cup (150 g) mixed berries, such as strawberries, raspberries, and blueberries

To make this simple "ice cream," all you need is the frozen fruit on standby and a food processor and you'll have a light, refreshing, sugar-free dessert in minutes.

Cut the bananas into ¾-inch (2-cm) thick slices and lay, slightly apart, on a baking sheet lined with baking parchment.

Hull the strawberries and place all the berries in a freezerproof container. Freeze the bananas and berries for at least 6 hours.

Tip the banana slices and berries into a food processor and process for 3 to 5 minutes, scraping down the sides of the bowl a few times, until the mixture is smooth and of a soft ice-cream consistency. Serve immediately.

Mango, coconut, and lime ice cream

Serves 4

1 large ripe mango

⅞ cup (200 ml) coconut milk

Finely grated zest and juice of 1 lime

This ice cream is made in moments from blended frozen mango and coconut milk. The only sweetness comes from the sticky, syrupy mango, so make sure you use one that is ripe.

Peel the mango, cut the flesh from the seed, then cut into coarsely ¾-inch (2-cm) chunks. Place in a freezerproof bowl and freeze for a minimum of 6 hours.

Pour the coconut milk into ice-cube trays and freeze for 2 to 3 hours, until firm and icy but not frozen solid.

Put the frozen mango, coconut milk cubes, and the lime zest and juice into a food processor and blend for about 5 minutes, scraping down the sides every so often, until the mixture if of a soft ice-cream consistency. Serve immediately.

 A balanced approach

Moderation and balance are key to any successful healthy diet. Avoiding specific foods on the basis that they are "bad for us" can be counterproductive. Ice creams and sorbets, for example, can form part of a balanced meal if you make them yourself and typically include fruit and other nutrient-rich ingredients. For a contrast in texture, if required, serve them with fresh fruit rather than dessert cookies with a high fat content.

Berry and rose water sorbet

Serves 4

1¾ cups (250 g) strawberries, hulled

2 cups (250 g) raspberries

¼ tsp rose water

2 tsp maple syrup

2 Tbsp water (if needed)

The subtle, floral aroma of rose water complements the natural sweetness of berries in this refreshing sorbet.

Halve scant 1 cup (150 g) of the strawberries and place these in a freezerproof container with all of the raspberries. Freeze for a minimum of 6 hours.

Once the fruit it completely frozen, transfer to a food processor and add the fresh strawberries, rose water, and maple syrup. Blend for about 5 minutes, scraping the sides down regularly, until you have a soft, spoonable sorbet.

If the mixture still seems very stiff after 5 minutes of blending, add 2 Tbsp water and blend again. Serve immediately.

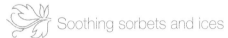 Soothing sorbets and ices

Sensitive gums and a sore mouth are a common consequence of cancer treatment and care must be taken to prevent localized infections, as your body has enough to cope with fighting cancer. Cold, smooth foods like ices and sorbets can provide a welcome relief from discomfort. Make your own soft ices and smoothies and use them as a means to introduce nutrient-rich fruits into your diet, remembering to avoid any ingredients known to irritate your mouth.

Pumpkin pie slices

Makes 16

For the filling

1 large butternut squash

7 Tbsp (100 ml) maple syrup

⅝ cup (150 ml) coconut milk

3 large eggs, beaten

2 tsp vanilla extract

1 tsp ground cinnamon

¼ tsp ground nutmeg

For the base

Scant 1 cup (100 g) pecan halves

¾ cup (75 g) ground almonds

⅓ cup (25 g) rolled oats

2 Medjool dates, coarsely chopped

1 large egg, beaten

This lovely traybake gives you all the warming flavours of a traditional pumpkin pie in a little slice. Once cooled, the slices can be kept in the refrigerator for 2 to 3 days.

Preheat the oven to 400°F (200°C).

Cut the squash in half, remove the seeds, and wrap each half in foil. Place in a roasting tray and bake in the oven for 1 to 1½ hours until completely tender. Remove from the oven, open up the foil, and set aside to cool.

Turn the oven down to 350°F (180°C). Lightly grease and line a 9-inch (23-cm) square shallow baking pan with baking parchment.

While the squash is cooling, prepare the base. Tip the pecans into a food processor and blitz for 2 to 3 minutes, until the nuts start to clump together. Add the remaining ingredients and blend to a fairly sticky dough.

Using wet hands, press the dough onto the base of the prepared pan as evenly as you can. Bake in the oven for 8 minutes, until beginning to turn golden. Remove and set aside to cool while you prepare the filling.

Scoop the cooled flesh from the squash; you should have about 600g. Spoon into the cleaned food processor, add the rest of the filling ingredients, and blend until smooth and creamy. Pass the mixture through a strainer and spread evenly over the base.

Bake in the oven for 25 to 30 minutes, until the filling is just set. Let cool and then chill to firm up before serving. Cut into 16 squares to serve.

Apple, almond, and cinnamon cake

Makes 12 slices

4 dessert apples

Juice of ½ lemon

½ cup (100 g) golden raisins, chopped fairly finely

2 Tbsp water

4 large egg whites

2 Tbsp maple syrup

Scant ½ cup (50 g) whole wheat all-purpose flour

Generous 1 cup (100 g) ground almonds

1 tsp ground cinnamon

1 tsp baking powder

2 Tbsp sunflower oil

This delicate cake is made with a maple meringue to keep it light and fluffy. Wrapping the hot cake in a dish towel as it cools helps to retain the delicious moisture from the fruits.

Preheat the oven to 350°F (180°C). Lightly grease a 7-inch (18-cm) springform cake pan and line with baking parchment.

Peel the apples and chop all but one into fairly small chunks. Quarter and core the other apple, then cut into fairly thin slices. Sprinkle all of the apple pieces with the lemon juice.

Put the chopped apples into a saucepan with the golden raisins and water. Place over medium-low heat and simmer gently for 10 to 15 minutes, stirring regularly, until the apples are fairly soft. Tip the mixture into a bowl and set aside to cool.

In a clean bowl, whisk the egg whites until they form stiff peaks. Trickle over the maple syrup and whisk again until stiff.

Sift the flour, ground almonds, cinnamon, and baking powder together over the egg whites, tipping in any bran and almonds that remain in the strainer. Carefully fold the flour and almond mixture into the meringue with a spatula or large metal spoon until just combined. Finally, fold in the cooled fruit.

Spoon the batter into the prepared pan and gently smooth the surface with a spatula. Arrange the apple slices on top of the cake in concentric circles. Bake in the oven for 30 to 35 minutes, until golden and a toothpick inserted into the center of the cake comes out clean.

Let the cake cool in the pan for 10 minutes before turning out. Wrap the warm cake in a dish towel as it cools and serve warm or at room temperature. Once cooled, it will keep for 2 to 3 days stored in an airtight container.

5 WAYS WITH *dried fruit*

Changes in taste perception following breast cancer treatment can lead to avoidance of acidic fresh fruits. Dried fruits offer a compact, easily transportable alternative with a multitude of uses. They have a concentrated, positive nutrient profile —containing valuable micronutrients, phytochemicals, and soluble fiber. Try these luscious suggestions to increase your intake.

Chocolate and date truffles
In a food processor, blitz ½ cup (100 g) pitted dates with ¾ cup (75 g) dry unsweetened coconut, ¾ cup (75 g) ground almonds, 4 Tbsp unsweetened cocoa, and 1 Tbsp melted coconut oil until mixture forms a dough. Roll into 16 balls and chill for 4 days.

Healthy fruit bars
Line a 9-inch (23-cm) square shallow baking pan with baking parchment. Blend 3½ oz (100 g) dried figs, ½ cup (100 g) dried apricots, 1 Tbsp melted coconut oil, and 1 cup (100 g) cashews until smooth, and spread in the pan. Chill for 2 hours, then slice into 16 bars.

Apricot paste
Put scant 1 cup (200 g) dried apricots in a bowl, pour on 1¼ cups (300 ml) boiled water, and soak for 30 minutes, until plump. Blend until smooth and use to sweeten cakes, yogurt—even salad dressings.

Cranberry roasted veg
Roast carrots, parsnips, and celeriac in a little olive oil and sprinkle with a spoonful of dried cranberries to serve.

Sticky prune oatmeal
Make oatmeal with ⅝ cup (50 g) rolled oats and 1 to 1¼ cups (250 to 300 ml) milk, and flavor with pinch of cinnamon. Chop 3 prunes and stir through the oatmeal to serve.

Drinks

Passion fruit and mint cooler

Serves 2

1 passion fruit

½ lime, cut into wedges

2 Tbsp mint leaves

Sparkling water, to top off

Crushed ice, to serve

This refreshing summer drink will be perfectly cooling on a hot summer's day.

Halve the passion fruit and scoop out the pulp and seeds with a teaspoon into a measuring cup. Add the lime wedges and mint leaves and lightly crush the ingredients together with a wooden spoon until juicy.

Half-fill two glasses with crushed ice and spoon over the crushed fruit and mint mix. Top off with sparking water, stir, and serve.

Watermelon, ginger, and lemon juice

Serves 4

1½ lb (750 g) watermelon flesh, cut into chunks

⅜-inch (1-cm) piece of fresh ginger, peeled

Juice of 1 lemon

The sweetness of watermelon is given an edge with spicy ginger and citrusy lemon.

Put the watermelon, ginger, and lemon juice in a food processor and blitz thoroughly. There is no need to remove the watermelon seeds first as blending will grind them down, but if you prefer a velvety smooth result, strain the juice before serving over ice.

Lemongrass, ginger, and lime infusion

Serves 2

1 lemongrass stalk

⅜-inch (1-cm) piece of fresh ginger, peeled and sliced

½ lime, cut into wedges

2½ cups (600 ml) boiling water

This aromatic blend is a wonderfully cleansing drink to enjoy first thing in the morning.

Bruise the lemongrass stalk with the back of a knife and slice in half. Divide the lemongrass, ginger, and lime between 2 large mugs and pour over the boiling water. Let infuse for 3 to 5 minutes before drinking.

Mayan almond hot chocolate

Serves 2

1¾ oz (50 g) good quality semisweet chocolate, minimum 60% cocoa solids, chopped into small pieces

½ teaspoon ground cinnamon

2 cups (500 ml) unsweetened almond milk

This luxurious drink combines the richness of semisweet chocolate with the warm spice of cinnamon for a real treat. Almond milk lends a sweet nuttiness.

Put the chocolate, cinnamon, and almond milk into a pan and place over medium-low heat. Whisk until the chocolate has melted and the milk is hot and frothy. Serve in large mugs.

5 WAYS WITH *flavored water*

Although it is possibly the most important thing we consume, water intake is typically a low priority. Use your brain (75% of which is water) and replace caffeinated beverages and fruit juices—often avoided by patients during chemotherapy—with some of these refreshing, low sugar alternatives.

Sparkling water with cucumber and mint
Slice ¼ cucumber and divide between 2 glasses. Add 2 Tbsp mint leaves and crush lightly with a spoon. Pour over ice-cold sparkling water and serve. 2 servings

Strawberry and basil water
Divide ¾ cup (100 g) halved, hulled strawberries and 2 Tbsp basil leaves between 2 large glasses and crush lightly with a spoon. Half-fill the glasses with ice cubes and top off with still or sparkling water. Stir and serve. 2 servings

Citrus and rosemary water
Put 3 lightly bruised rosemary sprigs, 1 sliced orange, and 1 sliced lemon in a large pitcher and top off with water until two-thirds full. Give it a good stir and let infuse for 30 minutes. Top off the pitcher with ice and serve. 4 servings

Apple and cinnamon infusion
Peel, core, and slice 3 dessert apples. Toss 8 apple slices in a little lemon juice to stop them discoloring; set aside. Put the rest of the apples in a saucepan, pour on 2¼ cups (550 ml) water, and add a cinnamon stick. Bring to a simmer over medium heat and simmer for 10 minutes, until the apples are soft and the water is nicely infused. Strain the hot water into mugs and serve topped with the remaining apple slices, as a winter warmer. 2 servings

Berry crush ice cubes
Take a handful of mixed berries, such as strawberries, blueberries, and raspberries, and cut any larger fruit into small chunks. Distribute half of the berries equally among 1 or 2 ice-cube trays. Lightly crush the remaining fruit with a fork and divide among the trays. Squeeze over some lemon juice, top off with water and freeze for at least 2 hours. Add a few of the fruity ice cubes to a glass of still or sparkling water for a refreshing infusion.

Bibliography

Diet and breast cancer, understanding risks and benefits Thomson CA. Nutrition in Clinical Practice, Oct 2012, 27(5), pp. 636–50.

WHO, 2014 Cancer: Fact sheet N°297. Available from World Health Organization: who.int/mediacentre/factsheets/fs297/en

Modification in the diet can induce beneficial effects against breast cancer Aragón F, Perdigón G, de Moreno de LeBlanc A. World Journal of Clinical Oncology, Aug 2014, 5(3), pp.455–64.

Significant changes in dietary intake and supplement use after breast cancer diagnosis in a UK multicentre study Velentzis LS, Keshtgar MR, Woodside JV, Leathem AJ, Titcomb A, Perkins KA et al. Breast Cancer Research and Treatment, July 2011, 128(2), pp.473–82.

Multi-professional management of patients with breast cancer Lewis M, Davies I, Cooper J. Available from Cancer Research UK: cancerresearchuk.org

Breast and cervical cancer in 187 countries between 1980 and 2010: a systematic analysis Forouzanfar MH, Foreman KJ, Delossantos AM, Lozano R, Lopez AD, Murray CJ, Naghavi M. Lancet, Oct 2011, 378(9801), pp.1461–84.

The incidence of breast cancer: the global burden, public health considerations Forbes, JF. Seminars in Oncology, 1997, 24(1), pp.20–35.

Epidemiology of breast cancer: an environmental disease? Sasco AJ, APMIS, May 2001, 109, pp.321–32.

Cancer incidence in five continents. Perkins DM. International Agency for Research on Cancer, Scientific Publication 1997, 7, pp.1–1240.

Estimates of worldwide burden of cancer in 2008 GLOBOCAN 2008 International. Ferlay J, Shin HR, Bray F, Forman D, Mathers C, Parkin DM. Journal of Cancer, Dec 2010, 127, pp.2893–2917.

Adherence to the Mediterranean diet and risk of breast cancer The European prospective investigation into cancer and nutrition cohort study. Buckland G, Travier N, Cottet V et al. International Journal of Cancer, June 2013, 132(12), pp.2918–2927.

Diet and breast cancer: a systematic review Mourouti N, Kontogianni MD, Papavagelis C, Panagiotakos DB. International Journal of Food Sciences and Nutrition, Feb 2015, pp.1–42.

Food, nutrition, physical activity and the prevention of cancer: a global perspective Washington DC. World Cancer Research Fund, American Institute for Cancer Research (AICR). AICR, 2007.

Physical activity and risk of breast cancer overall and by hormone receptor status The European prospective investigation into cancer and nutrition. Steindorf K, Ritte R, Eomois PP, Lukanova A et al. International Journal of Cancer, April 2013, 132(7), pp.1667–78.

Physical activity and health: a report of the Surgeon General US Dept of Health and Human Services, Centers for Disease Control and Prevention, National Center for Chronic Disease Prevention and Health Promotion, 1996.

Body mass index and survival in women with breast cancer Systematic literature review and meta-analysis of 82 follow-up studies. Chan DS, Vieira AR, Aune D, Bandera EV, Greenwood DC, McTiernan A et al. Annals of Oncology, Oct 2014, 10, pp.1901–14.

Weight change in middle adulthood and breast cancer risk The EPIC-PANACEA study. Emaus MJ, Van Gils CH, Bakker MF, Bisschop CN et al. International Journal of Cancer, Dec 2014, 135(12), pp.2887–99.

Effect of obesity and other lifestyle factors on mortality in women with breast cancer Prospective Analysis of Case-control studies on Environmental factors and health (PACE) study group. Maso LD, Zucchett A, Talamini R, Serraino D, Stocco CF, Marina Vercelli et al. International Journal of Cancer, Nov 2008, 123(9), pp.2188-94.

Links between alcohol consumption and breast cancer: a look at the evidence Liu Y, Nguyen N, Colditz GA. Women's Health (London England), Jan 2015, 11(1), pp.65–77.

Alcohol consumption and breast cancer survival: a meta-analysis of cohort studies Gou YJ, Xie DX, Yang KH, Liu YL, Zhang JH, Li B, He XD. Asian Pacific Journal of Cancer Prevention, 2013, 14(8), pp.478–90.

Breast cancer survival in African American women: Is alcohol consumption a prognostic indicator? Paige A, McDonald PA, Williams R, Dawkins F, Adams-Campbell Ll. Cancer Causes & Control, Aug 2002, 13, pp.543–9.

Moderate alcohol consumption during adult life, drinking patterns and breast cancer risk Chen WY, Rosner B, Hankinson SE, Colditz GA, Willett WC. Journal of the American Medical Association, Nov 2011, 306, pp.1920–1

Case-control study of phytoestrogens and breast cancer Ingram D, Sanders K, Kolybaba M, Lopez D. Lancet, Oct 1997, 350, pp.990–4.

Urinary phytoestrogen excretion and breast cancer risk among Chinese women in Shanghai Dai Q, Franke AA, Jin F, Shu XO, Cluster LJ, Cheng J et al. Cancer Epidemiology Biomarkers and Prevention, Sept 2002, 11, pp.815–21.

The DietCompLyf study: a prospective cohort study of breast cancer survival and phytoestrogen consumption Swann R, Perkins KA, Velentzis LS, Ciria C, Dutton SJ, Dwek MV et al. Maturitas, July 2013, 75(3), pp.232–40.

Dietary lignan intakes in relation to survival among women with breast cancer: the Western New York exposures and breast cancer study McCann SE, Thompson LU, Nie J et al. Breast Cancer Research and Treatment, July 2010, 122, pp.229–35.

Soy food intake and breast cancer survival Shu XO, Zheng Y, Cai H et al. Journal of the American Medical Association, Dec 2009, 302, pp.2437–43.

Differential influence of dietary soy intake on the risk of breast cancer recurrence related to HER2 status Woo HD, Park KS, Ro J, Kim J. Nutrition and Cancer, Jan 2012, 64, pp.198–205.

Phytoestrogens and prevention of breast cancer: the contentious debate Bilal I, Chowdhury A, Davidson J, Whitehead S. World Journal of Clinical Oncology, Oct 2014, 5(4), pp.705–12.

Soy food consumption and breast cancer prognosis Cancer Epidemiology Biomarkers and Prevention. Caan BJ, Natarajan L, Parker B, Gold EB, Thomson C, Newman V et al. Feb 2011, 20(5), pp.854–8.

Intake of dairy products, calcium and vitamin D and risk of breast cancer Shin MH, Holmes MD, Hankinson SE, Wu K, Colditz GA, Willett WC. Journal of the National Cancer Institute, Sept 2002, 94(17), pp.1301–11.

Intakes of calcium and vitamin D and breast cancer risk in women Lin J, Manson JE, Lee IM, Cook NR, Buring JE, Zhang SM. Archives of International Medicine, May 2007, 167(10), pp.1050–9.

Major food sources of calories, added sugars and saturated fats and their contribution to essential nutrient intakes in the US diet Huth et al. Nutrition Journal 2013, 12, p116 www.nutritionj.com/content/12/1/116

Effects of dietary fatty acid composition from a high fat meal on satiety Kozimor A et al. Appetite, Oct 2013, 69, pp.39–45 www.ncbi.nlm.nih.gov/pubmed/23688821

Plasma free 25-hydroxyvitamin D, vitamin D binding protein, and risk of breast cancer The Nurses' Health Study II. Wang J, Eliassen H, Spiegelman D, Willett WC, Hankinson SE. Cancer Causes Control, April 2014, 25(7), pp.819–27

Consumption of Antioxidant-Rich Beverages and Risk for Breast Cancer in French Women Hirvonen T, Mennen LI, de Bree A, Castetbon K, Galan P, Bertrais S et al. Annals of Epidemiology, July 2006, 16, pp.503–8.

Post-diagnosis dietary factors and survival after invasive breast cancer Beasley JM, Newcomb PA, Trentham-Dietz A, Hampton JM, Andrew J. Bersch, Michael N et al. Breast Cancer Research and Treatment, Jan 2011, 128(1), pp.229–36.

Nutritional analysis All recipes were analysed using NetWISP nutritional software version 4, © 2006-2015 Tinuviel Software

Breast Cancer.org
Breast cancer awareness and information
www.breastcancer.org

Breast Cancer Care
Information and support for anyone affected by breast cancer
www.breastcancercare.org.uk

Breakthrough Breast Cancer
Breast cancer research charity
www.breakthrough.org.uk

National Cancer Institute
US site offering information on breast cancer and treatment
cancerwww.cancer.gov/cancertopics/types/breast

Cancer Research UK
Charity raising funds for research into all forms of cancer
www.cancerresearchuk.org

Dana-Farber Cancer Institute
US cancer research organisation
www.dana-farber.org/

British Nutrition Foundation
Information and news of emerging food and nutrition related issues
www.nutrition.org.uk/

Dr Susan Love Research Foundation
US organisation providing information on breast cancer prevention, detection and treatment
www.dslrf.org/breastcancer

Susan G Komen
US charity funding breast cancer research and support
ww5.komen.org/BreastCancer/AboutBreastCancer.html

World Cancer Research Fund International
Continuous Update Project Report: diet, nutrition, physical activity and breast cancer survivors.
www.wcrf.org/sites/default/files/Breast-Cancer-Survivors-2014-Report.pdf

Recipe analysis and further information
www.westminster.ac.uk/breastcancercookbook
www.ucl.ac.uk/breastcancercookbook
www.royalfree.nhs.uk/breastcancercookbook

Index

Dedication

'I am grateful to all my breast cancer patients who inspired me to do this book.'

M. Keshtgar

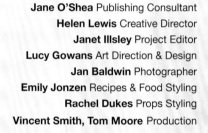

Jane O'Shea Publishing Consultant
Helen Lewis Creative Director
Janet Illsley Project Editor
Lucy Gowans Art Direction & Design
Jan Baldwin Photographer
Emily Jonzen Recipes & Food Styling
Rachel Dukes Props Styling
Vincent Smith, Tom Moore Production

Professor Mohammed Kestgar Faculty of Medical Sciences, University College London, and Consultant Breast Cancer Specialist, Royal Free Hospital London
Dr Claire Robertson Registered Nutritionist, University of Westminster
Dr Miriam Dwek Reader, Group Leader Breast Cancer Research Unit, University of Westminster

First published in 2016 by
Quadrille Publishing Limited
www.quadrille.co.uk

Quadrille is an imprint of Hardie Grant
www.hardiegrant.com.au

Cataloguing in Publication Data:
a catalogue record for this book is
available from the British Library.

ISBN 978 184949 839 5

Printed in China